WELLS-NEXT-THE-SEA
LIFEBOATS

WELLS-NEXT-THE-SEA
LIFEBOATS

NICHOLAS LEACH AND PAUL RUSSELL

TEMPUS

Frontispiece: Wells lifeboat Doris M. Mann of Ampthill *and inshore lifeboat*
Jane Ann II *entering harbour together. (Nicholas Leach)*

First published 2006

Tempus Publishing Limited
The Mill, Brimscombe Port,
Stroud, Gloucestershire, GL5 2QG
www.tempus-publishing.com

© Nicholas Leach and Paul Russell, 2006

British Library Cataloguing in Publication Data.
A catalogue record for this book is available from the British Library.

ISBN 0 7524 3875 1

Typesetting and origination by Tempus Publishing Limited.
Printed in Great Britain.

Contents

Acknowledgements

This book could not have been written without the extensive help and assistance of Coxswain Allen Frary whose support and helpfulness has known no bounds. He has provided a constant stream of information and been an enthusiastic supporter of the project since its inception. Together with crew member Bridget Marshall, he answered numerous questions and always supplied extra information whenever it was needed. Our gratitude to them both is considerable. Thanks are also due, in particular, to Campbell MacCallum, Wells station photographer, for his outstanding photos; Jeff Morris, David Gooch and Peter Edey for supplying photographs and illustrations; and to various members of RNLI staff at their headquarters in Poole for making facilities available for research. Jenny Sheldrake at the *Eastern Daily Press* and the staff at the Millennium Library at Norwich have also been of much assistance. A particular thanks to both Mick Bensley for allowing some of his excellent paintings to be reproduced, and to Nicky King, deputy second coxswain, for kindly providing his boat as a photo platform.

Wells lifeboat station as it is today with 12m Mersey Doris M. Mann of Ampthill *ready for launching. (Nicholas Leach)*

Introduction

The small town of Wells-next-the-Sea, a picturesque tourist spot on the north Norfolk coast and a small fishing port, can be divided into three parts: the quay, the old streets behind it, and the beach area a mile to the north. The small quay is a bustling jumble of cafés, amusement arcades and souvenir shops, and a number of former lifeboats under private ownership have been kept here over the years, mingling with the many small fishing boats. Along the quay is the first lifeboat house, now restored and used as the harbour master's office, with the lifeboat memorial on the opposite side of the road.

The current lifeboat station, situated at the beach, is an integral part of the town. The lifeboat, on its carriage ready to be launched over the beach at the mouth of the harbour, is an attraction to the many holiday-makers who travel to the town. The boathouse is usually open to visitors who can wander round, look at photos of crews past and present, read service boards listing the many rescues, and view the immaculately maintained lifeboat and its launching tractor.

The lifeboat crew, all volunteers with the exception of the coxswain/mechanic, devote much of their time to the lifeboat and are held in high esteem by all. In maintaining a tradition of life-saving that dates back to the early nineteenth century, the Wells lifeboat crew 'do not make judgements and do not question – they just go to the needy'. This

Two plaques at Wells Quay incorporated into a newly-built wall surrounding the old lifeboat house. On the left is a date roundel marking the date of the construction of the first lifeboat house and the establishment of the Wells lifeboat station; on the right is a date badge for the Port of Wells. (Nicholas Leach)

assessment, made by the Revd William Sayer at the annual lifeboat service, is as true now as it was when Wells first had a lifeboat. This volume is a tribute to all who have served the Wells lifeboat station and provides an account of how the service has developed and adapted over more than a century and a half.

Nicholas Leach, Birmingham, and Paul Russell, Cromer

December 2005

The Rescue Team: Wells lifeboat crew and station personnel photographed on 9 June 2002 with the other organisations involved behind the scenes, including the coastguards, lifeguards, police, fire, paramedics and RAF rescue helicopter from Wattisham. This image was used by the RNLI for promoting the lifeboat servuce. Not long after the photo was taken, the lifeboat was called out to the barge De Hoop 3 *which had lost an engine. (Campbell MacCallum)*

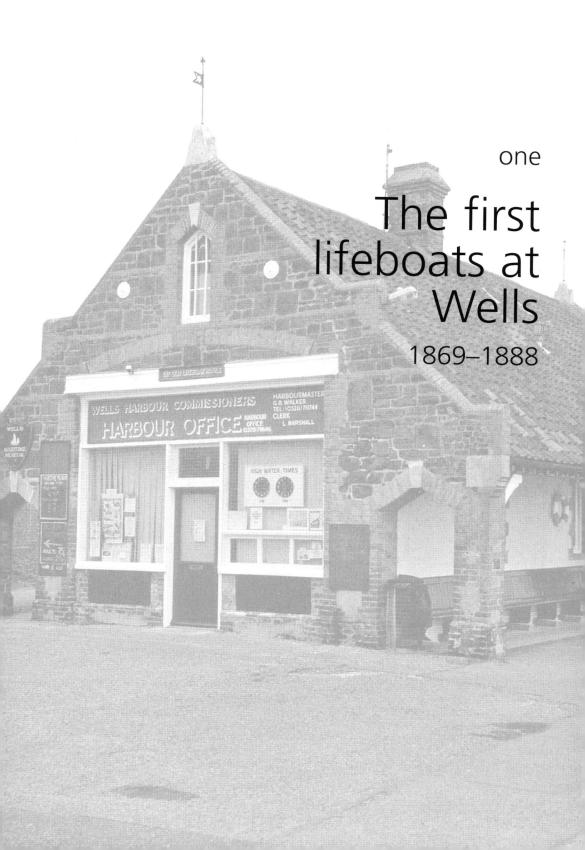

one

The first lifeboats at Wells

1869–1888

The early history of the lifeboat station at Wells-next-the-Sea is a little unusual in that the first lifeboat was supplied by an independent authority at a time when a national lifeboat organisation was in existence. That organisation, the Royal National Institution for the Preservation of Life from Shipwreck, was founded in 1824 and set about supplying lifeboats to stations around the coast. Before its formation, however, a number of local initiatives had come to fruition including one in Norfolk where the Norfolk Shipwreck Association (NSA) had funded lifeboats at strategic points along that coastline. The first lifeboat stationed at Wells was supplied in 1830 by the NSA after being transferred from Cromer, the station for which it was built in 1804. Although records of any rescues it performed have not been found, the Act for Improving the Harbour and Quay at Wells dated 29 July 1844 asserted that 'an efficient and well-appointed Life Boat, with all the necessary tackle and other requisites, and a competent crew for the effectual working thereof…stationed at or in the immediate vicinity of the Harbour and Quay' be maintained by the harbour commissioners. A further clause in the Act penalised the commissioners should they fail to provide the lifeboat by having to 'forfeit and pay the sum of Two pounds for every Twenty-four hours during which the said Life Boat . . . shall not be provided or maintained, or stationed as aforesaid'.

This lifeboat was included in the 1843 Parliamentary Report on Shipwrecks, which included a list of all lifeboat stations. The report stated that the boat was 'kept in a boat-house, near the entrance of Wells Harbour (west side)', adding that George Croft, Esq, of Wells, 'had the boat under his charge'. The boat was also in operation a decade later meriting a similar entry in the Duke of Northumberland's Report of 1851, which describes the lifeboat as 25ft by 8ft 6in, ten-oared and 'kept in a boat-house at the west side of the entrance to Wells Harbour'. The lifeboat was of the North Country type, similar to the first purpose-built lifeboats designed and built at South Shields by boatbuilder Henry Greathead in the late eighteenth century, but it is not known how long the station remained in operation after the report of 1851.

Whatever became of this lifeboat is not known. But while the national institution forged ahead, being reformed and renamed the Royal National Lifeboat Institution in 1854 and generating greater revenues to fund and expand the lifeboat fleet, the situation at Wells went into something of a decline. By the 1860s, no lifeboat was in operation on this part of the coast yet the frequency of wrecks was increasing. To remedy the situation, the RNLI were approached by local people with a view to establishing a station. In August 1868, the Inspector of Lifeboats visited the town to determine whether a lifeboat should be operated from Wells. He met the chairman of the harbour commissioners, Mr J.S. Southgate, Chief Officer of the Coastguard Lieut George E. Barnes, and the local Lloyd's agent, all of whom were in favour of the proposal. The Inspector then recommended to the RNLI's Committee of Management that a new station be formed, justifying his reasoning by stating that a considerable length of coast was without a lifeboat and vessels frequently went aground on the outlying sands.

The RNLI's committee agreed to this request and a standard 33ft ten-oared self-righting lifeboat was ordered for the new station. The self-righting type, first introduced in the 1850s, had gradually evolved during the latter half of the nineteenth century and the new boat at Wells

Going out for the first time on service, Eliza Adams *goes to the aid of the yacht* Stella *in August 1872. (From a painting by Mick Bensley)*

represented the latest advances in the design. Built from diagonally-planked Honduras mahogany with side and end air cases and an iron keel, she was 'painted blue and the bottom white, and a few inches from the top of the bulwarks is an off rim or fender, painted a bright red, and extending all round the boat, in which are slung ropes . . . of great assistance in saving life'.

To accommodate the new boat, a 'substantial' lifeboat house was built on the quay by Plowman & Son at a cost of almost £298 15s. The new house was described in *The Lifeboat* (the journal of the RNLI, first published in March 1852) as being at 'a convenient site in the town close to the residences of the men'. The boat could either be launched into the comparatively quiet waters of the harbour and rowed down the channel out to sea or taken by road to the shore, about a mile west of the harbour, and launched directly into the sea. The new house was funded from subscriptions raised in the immediate vicinity of the town to which the Earl of Leicester gave £50. In 1872, a look-out at the rear of the house was added for a further £50.

Funding for the new lifeboat had come from the proceeds of 'penny readings' in various parts of the country as part of a project started by E.B. Adams, a surgeon of Bungay, helped by Dr Short, of Walsham-le-Willows. The readings were given in eighteen different counties raising enough money to more than pay for the entire cost of the lifeboat. Of the amounts raised, Suffolk contributed £315, Norfolk £161, and Essex £72. Although the account in *The Lifeboat* reported that the new lifeboat was named *Penny Readings and Eliza Adams*, the first half of the name was never used and she was known throughout her career as *Eliza Adams*, after the wife of the originator of the 'penny readings' movement. An engraved brass plate affixed to one end of the air-boxes read:

The 'substantial' lifeboat house built on the quay at Wells in 1869 with the station's first lifeboat Eliza Adams *outside. This is the only known photograph of* Eliza Adams. *(Allen Frary collection)*

The cost of this lifeboat was contributed to the Royal National Lifeboat Institution through the medium of Penny Readings in different parts of the country, the organisation and collection of the fund having been assiduously originated and promoted by E.B. Adams, of Bungay, 1869.

The new lifeboat was sent from London to her new station by the Great Eastern Co. free of charge, arriving at Wells on 12 November 1869. At about 11.30 a.m., a procession formed at the railway station and escorted the boat to the boathouse on the harbour, where she was formally presented by Dr Adams and accepted by Captain Ward RN, Inspector of Lifeboats. In front of a large crowd, the Countess of Leicester named the boat, described in the *Norfolk Chronicle*: 'The Countess of Leicester christened the boat as it passed from its carriage into the water amidst deafening cheers, the band struck up "Rule Britannia", and the riflemen fired several volleys. The crew, who wore the safety dress, rowed up the river, and the boat was, with some difficulty, upset, to prove her self-righting properties'.

The new lifeboat had to wait almost three years before her first call, but then in the space of three months she helped three different craft. On 27 August 1872, she went to the yacht *Stella*, of London, which had requested help while riding at anchor in Holkham Bay in a northerly gale. The lifeboat was rowed down to the bar and towed, with some difficulty, by the steam tug *Olive Branch*, to the yacht. The yacht's seven occupants, which included the Hon Frederick Walpole MP, were rescued. As soon as these people had been landed at Wells, *Eliza Adams* was called on again, this time to assist the brig *Criterion*, of Arbroath, which was sinking on the Blakeney West Sands. The steam tug again towed the lifeboat over the bar, and she then sailed down to the wreck through very heavy seas. As soon as she neared the wreck, she anchored to windward and veered down towards the casualty. This procedure was repeated several times until all nine crew from the brig had been rescued, after which they were landed at Blakeney.

Wells Quay in the 1880s, with the steam tug Promise *on the right, and one brig, four schooners and three ketches alongside in the heyday of sail. This would have been the view from the lifeboat house of 1869. (From an old photo supplied by Allen Frary)*

Less than three months after these two rescues, *Eliza Adams* was out again. On 11 November 1872, she launched to the fishing lugger *Northumberland*, of Flamborough, which was ashore at Wells East Bight from where the crew of ten had managed to reach the beach. They were taken on board the lifeboat and brought to Wells through the heavy northerly gale. The next effective rescue performed by *Eliza Adams* at Wells took place on 12 September 1878 when she was launched to the fishing sloop *Sally*, of Wells, which was making for the harbour in a very heavy northerly gale when her mainsheet and boom gave way. She was driven onto the East Sands to where the lifeboat was towed by a local steam tug. The lifeboat went alongside the sloop and took off her crew of four.

After this routine service had been completed, the next call on the Wells lifeboat was to end in tragedy. Throughout that day on 29 October 1880, strong winds and heavy seas caused a series of vessels to be blown ashore on the sands near Wells. At about 9 a.m., three vessels went ashore on Holkham Beach – the brig *Violet*, of Whitby, bound for Shields in ballast; the brig *Lois*, of Littlehampton, also in ballast; and *Sharon's Rose*, of Whitby, from Shields bound for Dieppe with coal. The crews of *Violet* and *Lois* were hauled ashore through the breakers by lifelines fired from the beach but the crew of *Sharon's Rose* could not be saved. Despite the fact that ships were in trouble and the lifeboat was needed, she remained in her boathouse. The manager was absent and no one was available to organise a launch, although the fishermen and beachmen were ready to put out. The manager was the local Lloyd's agent and had gone to Holkham to attend the wrecks, when perhaps he should have ordered the lifeboat to put out. The *Eastern Daily Press* reported that 'The lifeboat house is situated at the junction of the Quay with the bank, and consequently is a long distance from the beach, and it is the opinion of many of the residents that the lifeboat ought to have been got out of the harbour down to the shore two or three hours before it reached Holkham'.

At about midday, George Everett, one of the lifeboat's trustees, did order the lifeboat to launch but the crew had to row against a flowing tide and the lifeboat did not reach the first wrecked vessel until 1 p.m. She succeeded in saving the ship's seven crew who were by then in danger of being drowned. According to the newspaper's account, the lifeboat 'behaved splendidly while engaged in this service. Many times she was half filled with water, which flowed out instantly'. The steam tug *Promise*, which had been standing off throughout, then towed the lifeboat with the rescued crew into the harbour. But as soon as the lifeboat had returned, a vessel east of the harbour mouth and about three miles away, was seen flying distress signals. The crew volunteered to go out again, despite being wet and tired and with other crew keen to replace them. The lifeboat was again towed by the steam tug and found the brig *Ocean Queen*, stranded on the east high sand. The tug took the lifeboat to within about half a mile of the casualty and, watched by a large crowd who lined the quay and the bank, cast her off. But as the water was too shallow for the lifeboat to get near enough, the lifeboat crew rowed their boat back out to sea, anchored her and then set the sail. The brig's crew were okay and later walked ashore at low water.

A few minutes after *Eliza Adams* set off under sail to return to Wells, as she passed through the East Bight, she was caught in very heavy seas which capsized her with tragic consequences. One of the crew on board her, Thomas Kew, later recalled what happened: 'A sea broke quite over the top of the boat and fell into her. It was a tremendous sea. It turned the boat quite over'. As the lifeboat did not right herself for several minutes but drifted bottom up, much to the alarm of the onlookers, another boat was quickly manned and went to try to rescue the lifeboat crew. This other boat was taken out of the harbour and her crew of twelve landed on the east sands, running down to the line of breakers. By the time they reached the scene, the lifeboat, with masts broken, had moored herself as the anchor had fallen out and stuck in the ground. Although all had been wearing life-jackets when the lifeboat capsized and they were thrown into the water, they were unable to regain the boat when she righted because of their heavy boots and clothes. Thomas Kew managed to get ashore exhausted but alive and was pulled ashore by two men 'for he was powerless to rise', according to the *Eastern Daily Press* account. Another man, William Bell, was trapped in the lifeboat but was freed by the same men who had helped Kew ashore and, although found to be badly injured, also survived. Apart from these two, the other eleven in the crew lost their lives and their bodies were recovered during the next day or so.

Those who died were Captain Robert William Elsdon, 62, the harbour master, Coxswain John Elsdon, 60, fisherman; Samuel Smith, 33, fisherman; Charles Smith, brother of Samuel; William Field, 33, fisherman; George Jay, 46, fisherman; William Green, 56, pilot; Charles Hines, 30, sailor; John Stacey, 21, sailor; Francis Abel, 26, fisherman; and William Wordingham, 29, sailor. They left behind ten widows and twenty-seven children in a disaster described at the time as 'by far the most fatal accident that had ever befallen a Life-boat belonging to the National lifeboat Institution, the number of lives ever before lost, on any one occasion, having been six'.

Following the tragedy, which 'has carried sorrow into many a home, and cast a gloom over the town', a Fund for the Relief of the Widows and Orphans was set up with the aim of raising money for the bereaved. The RNLI gave £1,000 and Edward Birkbeck, MP for North Norfolk, offered his full support. In a letter to the *Norfolk Chronicle* of 6 November 1880 he wrote:

> of the gallant lifeboat men who perished from the Wells lifeboat…my present object is simply to ask your co-operation in helping me to bring the claims of the bereaved families under the notice of the public… The district in which the calamity occurred is a poor one, and…I therefore appeal… to bring into prominent notice the strong and urgent claims of the widows and orphans of those noble men who sacrificed their own lives…I beg to add that I shall be happy myself to receive contributions on behalf of the Fund.

Eliza Adams *goes alongside the Whitby brig* Sharon's Rose *during the storm of 29 October 1880. (From a painting by Mick Bensley)*

Eliza Adams *goes to the aid of the brig* Ocean Queen, *bound from Southampton to Seaham in ballast, on the lifeboat's last fateful mission, 29 October 1880. (From a painting by Mick Bensley)*

Thomas Kew, one of the two survivors of the disaster, standing next to the memorial which was unveiled on 12 September 1906. The memorial was built twenty-six years after the disaster when Thomas Kew returned to the town and made an appeal for something to be done to commemorate the men who gave their lives.
(Supplied by Allen Frary)

The funeral of the ten lifeboatmen was held on 3 November when all were interred in the cemetery apart from Charles Smith, whose body was never found. The first coffin was that containing the remains of Captain Elsdon, which was followed by his bereaved widow, relatives, and friends. The others were carried in succession, the mourners and friends each following their respective relatives. Next came the representatives of the public boards and institutions in the town, including the Wells improvement commissioners, harbour commissioners, and school board, and these were followed by most of the members of the Relief Committee and numbers of the public. The principal establishments of the town were closed, and many of the tradesmen were present. The burial service was conducted by the Revd J.R. Pilling, the Revd A. Napier (Holkham), the Revd E.R. Kerslake (Burnham), and the Revd A. Waller (Hunstanton). The church was not large enough to hold all the mourners with estimates suggesting that more than 2,000 persons were present.

An inquiry into the disaster was held to ascertain the cause of the capsize. One of the survivors, Thomas John Kew, gave evidence at the inquest, describing the events to Captain Napean RN, District Inspector of Lifeboats, with the aid of a model of the lifeboat, 'to get a perfect understanding of the matter'. Kew explained that when the boat capsized, she turned bottom upwards and came up on her beam ends on the other side, with sails floating on the water, and then drifted on her side as far as her anchor cable would allow. She then turned bottom up again, her mast having broken when it struck the ground, righted herself and rode at anchor which had fallen out when she capsized, with her head to sea and mizzen standing. He said that they were in an unbroken sea when they set sail, but believed they could not have reached the harbour with just oars. He also stated that the boat behaved very well and that the course taken had the full backing of the crew.

The explanation that the wet sails held down the boat prevailed; but Kew's explanation that the end of the mast went into the sand so the boat could not regain its proper position until it gave way seems more probable. There seems no reason for supposing that the boat would not have righted had she not been under sail; but with a crew, the greater part of whom had already been out on service, proceeding under sail was less an easier course of action than using the oars. The jury at the inquest concluded that 'the deceased were accidentally drowned by the capsizing of a lifeboat', adding that 'there was a little want of judgement shown by the crew in not making fast the anchor and throwing off the fore halliards'.

Wells was without a lifeboat from 29 October until early December 1880 when an unnamed boat was sent to the station to take the place of *Eliza Adams*, which was condemned and returned to London, either to the RNLI's storeyard at Poplar or to the builder Woolfe's yard, during 1881. The new lifeboat, which was carried to the station on board the steamship *Erasmus Wilson* free of charge, was later appropriated to the legacy of Charlotte Nicholls, of Finsbury Park. The boat had been built at a cost of £430 by Woolfe & Son of Shadwell. On 26 July 1882, she was 'publicly named and launched', as *The Lifeboat* of 1 November 1882 explained. The executors of Miss Nicholls estate wanted the lifeboat to be stationed on the English coast between the Thames and the Tees, and the money was subsequently appropriated for Wells. The practice of

The memorial, at the west end of the quay, to the eleven lifeboat men who were lost in October 1880. Close to the lifeboat house of 1869, it is on the landward side of the road to the beach. Restoration work in 2004 involved the brickwork at the base being replaced and the memorial itself being cleaned. (Nicholas Leach)

Wells' second lifeboat, Charlotte Nicholls, *during the only service she performed while at Wells, to the schooner* Emma, *of Jersey, on 4 October 1883. (From a painting by Mick Bensley)*

retrospectively giving names to unnamed new lifeboats was not uncommon in the nineteenth century. The boat, a 37ft twelve-oared self-righting type, was christened by Mrs Cocking, wife of the acting executor of the late Miss Nicholls, and dedicated by the Revd J.R. Pilling. Following the ceremony, 'A capital launch was effected, and as there was a strong breeze of wind, sails were hoisted, and the boat was displayed to good advantage before the numerous spectators', as the *People's Weekly Journal* reported. The committee retired to the Crown Hotel for refreshments and in the evening the crew had a dinner there provided at the expense of Mr and Mrs Cocking.

Charlotte Nicholls only performed one effective service during her seven years at the station. On 4 October 1883, she launched to the schooner *Emma*, of Jersey, which was stranded on the East Bar in a heavy north-easterly gale and heavy seas. The lifeboat launched soon after 10 p.m., and the lifeboatmen reached the casualty to find her sails torn, her bulwarks washed away and the heavy seas breaking over her. Five persons were on board, one of whom was a boy, and all were 'nearly dead with cold', as the official account explained. They were soon taken off by the lifeboat which landed them at Wells.

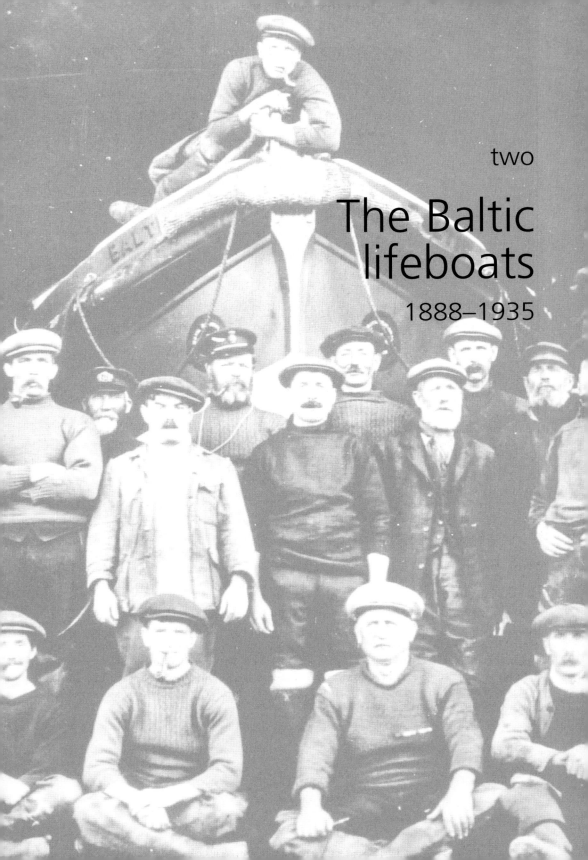

two

The Baltic lifeboats

1888–1935

In June 1887, the self-righting ability of *Charlotte Nicholls* was brought into question and, although the boat was less than seven years old at the time, a new boat was built for the station incorporating 'all the latest improvements'. The new lifeboat, sent to Wells in August 1888 via the Glasgow and South Western and Midland Railways, was funded from a collection made by H. Kains-Jackson at the London Corn Exchange. Kains-Jackson had collected 'a handsome sum each Christmas' in aid of the Gorleston lifeboat *Mark Lane*. The 1887 collection was so successful, raising more than £700 after being supplemented by a special collection from the Baltic Lifeboat Fund, that sufficient funds were available to fund the new Wells lifeboat as well, which was named *Baltic*. The boat, 37ft in length, twelve-oared and equipped with two masts, standing lugs and a jib, was built by D.W. Henderson & Co, of Partick, at the cost of £563 6s 6d and was 'of the latest self-righting class'. A launching carriage was sent from London via the Great Eastern Railway, free of charge, and *Charlotte Nicholls* was sold locally.

This first *Baltic* lifeboat lasted less than ten years at Wells and never undertook any effective services. Her short career and lack of effective life-saving acts can largely be attributed to the location of the boathouse at the town's quay, more than a mile from the sea, which in effect considerably reduced the boat's range. The difficulties were highlighted by a series of events in November 1893 when she launched to three different casualties but failed to effect any rescues. The first took place on the afternoon of 18 November when she put out from the town in force twelve northerly winds to the collier *Duke of Cornwall* which had gone ashore between Wells and Blakeney. Unable to make headway against wind and tide as the gale was so severe, the lifeboatmen, under the command of Captain Hinson, could not offer any assistance. The casualty was wrecked although her crew of three were saved by local coastguards. In the evening of the same day, another vessel got into difficulty. The barge *Lord Beresford*, carrying barley for Burnham Overy, anchored in Wells Bay but both anchors parted during the evening and the barge was driven ashore at Holkham Beach forcing her crew to take to the rigging. Although the lifeboat was again unable to assist, her crew were saved and she was later refloated.

Two days later, the lifeboat failed yet again to provide assistance. On this occasion, the schooner *Hickman*, bound from Rochester to the Firth of Forth with a cargo of cement, went ashore on the Bar at about 11 a.m. after her anchor cables parted. As soon as news of the casualty reached the town, *Baltic* was manned but the low tide prevented her from reaching the scene until about 1 p.m. She then dropped anchor but this dragged and the lifeboat was driven to leeward of the wreck. Despite many attempts, the lifeboatmen could not get their boat to windward of the schooner although remained within hailing distance. Two of the lifeboat crew, Alfred Fuller and Richard Whittaker, were washed overboard while the lifeboat was at anchor but fortunately both were recovered. The lifeboat was eventually beached having failed to help the *Hickman's* crew, who took to the rigging where they remained for several hours. Help was eventually provided by the salvage boat *Friends* which, with great difficulty, succeeded in saving the captain and two seamen after they had spent more than three hours attempting to get close to the casualty. The mate and the lad died from exposure in the rigging.

Following this tragedy, a witness of the events wrote to the *Eastern Daily Press* describing the situation and calling for a remedy: 'there is a schooner just ashore. In the harbour there is the

Naming ceremony of the second Baltic *lifeboat on the beach at Wells. (Wells Maritime Museum)*

The second Baltic *lifeboat being pulled across the beach by a team of horses. Before tractors were used, the effort required to launch the lifeboat was considerable and horses were usually employed to help. (Wells History Society)*

lifeboat with all the men fully equipped anxious to save life, but unable to get out, as there is no water. Surely the time has come for subscribers to know why the boathouse was not built on the beach. Here we have a new boat with patent apparatus to fix on the wheels to enable them to cross the sands, and all this fully a mile and a half from them and no road down…The lifeboat house is on the beach at Brancaster and Blakeney, and why not here'. At the inquest into the loss of life during the incident, the schooner's captain, William Pollock, believed 'the lifeboat was too light for the work, and very undandy at sea' despite the lifeboat crew doing their utmost to offer help.

The events of November 1893 highlighted major deficiencies at the station. As the lifeboat could not clear the harbour in certain winds to get to sea, even with a favourable tide, the

The second Baltic *on service to the ketch* Hopewell, *of Lynn, on 4 August 1900. The ketch was bound for Wells from Hull with a cargo of corn when she got caught out by bad weather in Holkham Bay. (From a painting by Mick Bensley)*

honorary secretary Herbert Loynes suggested that the lifeboat house should be moved to the Point overlooking the harbour mouth, about a mile and a quarter north of the first boathouse. This would obviate the need to row out of the harbour and also make low water launching possible without taking the boat four or five miles overland to Holkham Beach. In December 1893, a decision was made to move the station to the new location and, with the full backing of the local committee and crew, plans were drawn up for a new boathouse. In April 1894, the RNLI acquired the lease of the site for the new lifeboat house and a month later drawings and specifications were prepared 'for an inexpensive house to accommodate the new lifeboat'. During 1894 and 1895, the new house, complete with pile foundations and a slipway onto the beach, was constructed by local builder Mr J. Platten at a cost of £551 10s. The house took longer than anticipated to be built and on several occasions the RNLI architect visited the station to move the construction work forward. In fact, not until October 1895 – almost a year after it should have been finished – was the building ready with the builder having failed to complete his contract and an extra £53 10s 3d incurred for additional work.

Once the new boathouse was ready, however, a new lifeboat was sent to the station because not only did the events of November 1893 show the station's location to be inadequate but also suggested that the 1888-built *Baltic* was ineffective. The crew expressed their dissatisfaction with her, preferring a boat of the type then in use at the nearby Cromer and Blakeney stations, known as the Cromer type. Towards the end of 1894, the crew's wishes were granted when the RNLI ordered a new boat of the Cromer non-self-righting type from Beeching Bros of Great Yarmouth. This design, based on the 1830-built lifeboat at Cromer, was preferred by that

The 'substantial' lifeboat house built in 1869 on the quay, about a mile from the sea, in 1869 for the station's first lifeboat. One of many lifeboat houses built during the second half of the nineteenth centuury along similar lines, it was designed by the RNLI's architect, Charles Cooke and built from carstone, the only indigenous stone in this part of Norfolk.

After the lifeboat had been moved to a new boathouse in 1895, the 1869 boathouse built on the quay was presented to Wells Urban Council by the harbour commissioners for use as a reading room. The council bought the house in three yearly installments between 1896 and 1898 and since then it has since had a variety of uses. It was converted into the Jubilee Café in the 1960s but retained its general appearance with a symmetrical façade and covered aisles on each side. (Grahame Farr, courtesy of the RNLI)

station's crew in 1884 who had rejected the RNLI's self-righting design. The boat built for Wells was 35ft 3in in length, 10ft 3in in beam and 4ft 5in amidships. Clench built and pulled by fourteen oars, it was fitted with ten relieving tubes, three water ballast tanks, and a cork wale, and weighed almost four tons overall. Although completed in 1894 at the cost of £450, and taken into service on 8 January 1895, she was not sent to Wells until 16 July 1895 because of the delays in completing the new boathouse. A new carriage was supplied by Glover & Sons of Warwick and the old lifeboat and its carriage were returned to London.

Because the move to the beach – more than a mile and a quarter from the town – increased the time it took the crew to reach the lifeboat, the honorary secretary wrote to the RNLI in November 1895 on behalf of the coxswain, crew and helpers requesting an increase in pay. He stated that the crew wanted to receive the same amount of pay as the Blakeney and Brancaster crews, who lived a similar distance from the boathouses at their stations. The RNLI decided to comply with the request and placed the crew on same footing as those at Brancaster with the coxswain receiving £10 10s a year, consisting of a £9 salary and £1 10s tank allowance.

The new lifeboat, which like her predecessor was named *Baltic*, launched on service thirteen times and is credited with saving fifteen lives during her time at Wells. The first service she performed took place on 23 March 1898 after the fishing smack *F.T.B.*, of Boston, had got into difficulty in very heavy seas and a strong gale. At 5 p.m. the lifeboat was launched and took off the smack's crew of four who were brought ashore three hours later. *Baltic* performed her second service on 4 August 1900 when she was launched to the ketch *Hopewell*, of Lynn. The ketch had arrived in Holkham Bay on the afternoon of 3 August, just after high water, and waited for the next tide so she could proceed to the quay. While she was at anchor, the weather worsened and a heavy gale sprung up at about 10 p.m. The vessel dragged her two anchors and went ashore on the East bar at about 4 a.m., with the master and crew of two being forced to take to the rigging. Visibility was so poor because of the heavy rain that the stranded ship was not seen until about 8 a.m. *Baltic* was immediately launched and, on reaching the Scalp Beacon, was taken in tow by the steam tug *Marie*, which took the lifeboat to windward of the wreck. The lifeboat then sailed down to the casualty and, with some difficulty succeeded in rescuing the exhausted men. One of the lifeboatmen was washed overboard but came up on the leeward side and was immediately grabbed by his companions and pulled back on board. Following this service, a letter was received by the honorary secretary from R.W. Green, one of the men saved from the ketch, 'conveying our heart-felt thanks to the Wells [lifeboat]… Had it not been for the promptness in launching and the skilful handling of the boat by Coxswain Crawford and crew, I feel assured the result must have been different'.

During the opening years of the twentieth century, the Wells lifeboat was called on to perform a series of routine services. On 14 November 1901, the ketch *Lily*, of Grimsby, got into difficulty in a strong northerly gale and very heavy seas close to Bridgirdle Flat. *Baltic* was launched at 9 a.m. and succeeded in rescuing the ketch's crew of two. During 1902, she did not complete any effective services, although in October and November the crew were assembled in readiness to launch before being stood down as the vessels thought to be in difficulty required no assistance. Her only launch of 1903 took place on 11 September when the ketch *Eliza Patience,* of Great Yarmouth, went ashore on Holkham Beach in a northerly gale. *Baltic* was launched at 8.10 a.m. and saved the ketch's crew of two.

Almost six years passed before *Baltic* undertook another effective service, although she did put out to the sloop *Olive*, of Boston, on 14 December 1907 without rendering any assistance. During 1909, she was called out on three occasions making this her busiest year. On 1 April she was launched to the ketch *Providence*, of Goole. Bound from Hull to Wells with a cargo of oil cake, the ketch parted her anchors off the bar during a strong north-north-easterly gale. On

The new lifeboat house built on the beach in 1894/5 with the second Baltic lifeboat ready to be hauled out, August 1905. (By courtesy of Allen Frary)

The beach at the end of Beach Road, about a mile north of the quay, where the lifeboat house was built in 1894–5 for the second Baltic lifeboat. The house was similar in appearance to that built at Blakeney, to the east of Wells, and remains in use, having been extensively rebuilt for ever larger motor lifeboats. (From an old postcard supplied by David Gooch)

reaching the vessel, the lifeboat crew realised that saving it would be impossible because of the very heavy seas and its position close to the shore. The crew of four were rescued, however, and landed on Holkham Beach, after which the vessel became a total wreck. The next service was completed on 1 December when *Baltic* landed three from the barge *Jane*, of London, which was stranded on the East Point in rough seas. And on 22 December, the third and final service of the year involved *Baltic* saving the ketch barge *Davenport*, of Ipswich, and her crew of four after they became stranded at Burnham Overy in a moderate easterly gale.

The 1894-built *Baltic* remained at Wells until September 1913 by when she was regarded as out-dated and was condemned as unfit following an overhaul. At a meeting on 16 July 1913, Lieut Basil Hall RN, divisional inspector of lifeboats, explained to the local committee that the lifeboat had been condemned and a new boat would be built for the station in the near future. He went on to explain that because no new lifeboat had yet been built, the 35ft Liverpool type *James Stevens No.8* (ON.425), recently replaced at Ardrossan, was to be sent to replace *Baltic*. Built in 1899 in Scotland, this fourteen-oared boat had been replaced at her Ayrshire station and was thus available for Wells, being known as *Reserve 9B* during her time in Norfolk.

James Stevens No.8 arrived at Wells Quay on 15 October 1913 and, according to the *Eastern Daily Press*, 'aroused considerable interest, and a number of spectators gathered around to watch the operation of unloading the boat from the GER trucks. This was accomplished without a hitch under the direction of Rigger J. Martin and Coxswain T. Stacey'. The newspaper went on to say that, 'the newly arrived lifeboat was almost a new boat, was fitted with many

Lifeboat crew and helpers with the third Baltic *lifeboat in the lifeboat house on the beach. (By courtesy of Allen Frary)*

The second Baltic *being rowed towards Bridgirdle Flat where the ketch* Lily *was in difficulty, November 1901. (From a painting by Mick Bensley)*

modern improvements, [and] was the object of much admiration as she lay on the quay on Wednesday, prior to being taken to the lifeboat house on the beach on Thursday morning's tide'. *James Stevens No.8* was launched on exercise for the first time on the afternoon of 25 October 1913 and taken up the harbour towards the town. Lieut Hall and Thomas Readwin, a member of the local committee, accompanied the crew while a small crowd gathered on the beach to watch proceedings. The boathouse had to be altered for the new boat, which was longer than her predecessor, and these alterations cost £76 13s 3d.

Although *James Stevens No.8* was only a temporary lifeboat, she ended up staying at Wells for three years. During this time, she launched on service only twice, and saved no lives. In December 1914, a new pulling lifeboat was offered to the station and the following month the local committee, coxswain and crew requested that a Liverpool type boat, 38ft in length, similar to *James Stevens No.8* be supplied. The RNLI complied with this request and ordered a new lifeboat, from S.E. Saunders' yard at Cowes, with two drop keels, two water ballast tanks, modified No.1 rig and pulling fourteen oars. But with construction work dominated by the needs of the war, the new lifeboat was not ready until September 1916. She was then taken by steamer from Southampton to the Thames, where she was placed in the water. She was towed to Lowestoft with a navigating crew on board, and from Lowestoft sailed round the coast to Wells. *James Stevens No.8* was returned to London and the Reserve Fleet, serving until being condemned and sold in 1920.

In July 1916, the new boat was allocated the name *Baltic*, appropriating her to the donors of the previous lifeboat in recognition of the support from the Baltic Shipping Exchange over many years. The boathouse was altered with the plates on the floor moved and lengthened to accommodate a new carriage supplied by the Bristol Wagon Works at a cost of £353, together with a set of launching poles. Although she was not called upon for services until the war was over, the new *Baltic* was exercised a number of times with the inspector, Commander Hall, reporting that she 'sailed beautifully and…was admirably trimmed'.

The Wells lifeboat was hardly called upon during the First World War, but the war itself had an impact on the station. Conscription affected the numbers available to crew the boat and, during 1916, the District Inspector reported insufficient men were available should the lifeboat be required. The problems continued during 1917 when, in July following an exercise using horses for launching, the inspector reported that 'in the near future there would be difficulty

Two photographs showing the second Baltic *lifeboat being launched from her carriage with the lifeboat crew wearing cork life-jackets. The boat was of an unusual design, one of only three such lifeboats built. (Supplied by Allen Frary)*

The third Baltic *lifeboat being launched from her carriage. The Tipping's plates fitted to the main wheels were designed to prevent the carriage getting stuck in the soft sand and the drogue can be seen at the stern. (Wells Maritime Museum)*

getting a crew for the lifeboat'. This problem affected many stations in East Anglia, and may explain why the lifeboat was used so little. Only by July 1919 was a full crew available but launching arrangements were described 'as good as practicable,…horses were not obtainable for an exercise'.

Not only were shortages of crew a problem, but during the latter half of the war both the station and the groynes, which helped to maintain the beach, were damaged by soldiers stationed in the area. Despite RNLI requests to the military authorities in November 1916 to stop soldiers causing further damage, the officers in charge refused to give any guarantees. By February 1917, the boathouse had been locked so that it could not be used by the troops who occupied the annex. No further damage was caused by the soldiers, but exposure did cause the groynes to rot and the RNLI had to pay almost £50 for repairs, the replacement of the wooden faggots round the boathouse which retained the sand and renewal of the piles which supported the house. As the war drew to a close in late 1918, the boathouse was vacated by the military, but the necessary repairs had to be made and for which, in May 1919, the War Office paid £22.

The first service performed by the third *Baltic* lifeboat took place almost three years after she had first arrived at Wells. On 14 August 1919, at 1 p.m., she launched to the fishing boat *Rock of Ages*, which was in difficulty about seven miles off the harbour in a northerly gale and rough seas. The lifeboat assisted to save the boat and its crew of three. Less than two months later she was called out again, this time to of the steamship *Urd*, of Swansea, on 9 October in a strong gale, from which she saved the crew of six. *Baltic* was not called upon again for another two years. On 3 November 1921, she was launched at 7 p.m. to escort the motor fishing boat *Boy Robert*, of Wells, into harbour in rough seas. Her next launch was to the steamship *Coniscrag*, of Glasgow, on 4 September 1924. She put out at 6.50 a.m. into a strong north-north-easterly breeze and rough seas and assisted the ship, returning to station at 10.30 a.m.

The third Baltic *lifeboat on the beach, probably on lifeboat day with holiday-makers and visitors looking on.*

The last two services performed by *Baltic*, and indeed the last services by a pulling lifeboat at Wells, were both to the same casualty, the local motor fishing boat *Tony*. On 2 March 1934, she launched at 7.30 p.m. to the fishing boat which had not returned with the rest of the boats in the evening. Her owner was the lifeboat coxswain, and he and two other men were on board. After some time spent searching, the lifeboat crew saw a flare and at 10 p.m. the lifeboat found *Tony* about five miles off Wells, at anchor, with her engine broken down. The lifeboat towed her for a short time until a motor boat took over the tow back to harbour. The second service to *Tony* took place on 25 February 1935. After putting to sea in the morning, the vessel was caught out in worsening weather. As Cley coastguard, who reported that they had seen her going towards Blakeney, had lost sight of her, *Baltic* was launched at 3.15 p.m. in a moderate gale with very heavy seas and found *Tony* about half a mile north-north-west of the harbour unable to enter the harbour because of the conditions. The lifeboat rescued the three men, and towed the boat towards Burnham Overy in an endeavour to find a smooth place to beach her. However, the tow broke and she went ashore on the beach at Burnham after which the lifeboat made for home. This service was notable as it was the last in the United Kingdom to involve the use of horses for launching the lifeboat

A year after this service, Wells received a new motor lifeboat and *Baltic* became the Aldeburgh No.2 lifeboat for a further four years. After no service launches during her time at Aldeburgh, she was taken out of service and sold in December 1943 to a Mr H.L. Goodson, of Aldeburgh who renamed her *Marvin*. She has since had many different owners but was last reported at Southampton, with her original name back, in a somewhat derelict state of repair.

three

Royal Silver
Jubilee
1910–1935
1935–1945

Motor lifeboats first entered service with the RNLI in the early 1900s and, although a new motor lifeboat was not sent to Wells until 1936, the idea of such a craft for the station had first been mooted more than twenty-five years previously after the collier *Heathfield* had sunk between Blakeney and Sheringham in October 1910. She went down about two miles south-east of the West Sheringham Buoy and the bodies of the ten crew members who drowned were washed up on the beach at Wells. They were buried in the cemetery where a memorial was erected in their memory. Following this tragedy, the Divisional Inspector considered placing a motor lifeboat at Wells in June 1911 but the idea proved unworkable because insufficient water at all states of tide for such a lifeboat to lie afloat meant it would frequently be unable to get out of harbour. As the early designs of motor lifeboat had to be kept afloat, this ruled out Wells where carriage launching was the only viable method of launching.

But in October 1913, the idea of placing a motor lifeboat at the station was again raised when *James Stevens No. 8* arrived. At a meeting of the local committee, the 'advisability of accepting the offer of the RNLI of a motor lifeboat for the station' was discussed. Divisional Inspector Lieut Hall explained that carriage-launched motor lifeboats were still being developed, and 'strongly advised the committee to await the result of these experiments before definitely deciding whether or not to have a motor lifeboat at Wells'. With the First World War intervening in the RNLI's motor lifeboat development programme, the first carriage-launched motor lifeboats did not enter service until the 1920s and not until the 1930s was a design suitable for service at Wells available. Then, a small, light 32ft lifeboat ideal for launching from a beach was allocated to the station. This lifeboat was one of only nine boats of the non-self-righting Surf type to be built. The Surf class, designed by James Barnett, was light enough, weighing just three and a half tons, for launching from a carriage, manhandling across a beach and, with a small draught, working in shallow water. When introduced, it was the only twin-engined lifeboat type capable of being carriage launched, and carried two oars but no auxiliary sails. Because she was not intended to be at sea for more than a few hours, no shelter for crew protection was fitted.

The most notable feature of the new craft was her innovative system of propulsion. While the first Surf lifeboat *Rosabella* (ON.779), stationed at Ilfracombe, was powered by screw propellers, the second boat, which came to Wells, ON.780, was driven by the Hotchkiss Internal Cone coupled to 12hp engines built by Weyburn Engineering to an RNLI design. The Hotchkiss Cone system was basically an early form of water-jet which drew water through an opening and propelled it out of another. This method of propulsion had several advantages over the propeller, particularly in a vessel of shallow draft. At Wells, where the close-lying sandbanks necessitated a protected propeller, the cones were considered ideal while the boat's light weight meant carriage launching could be easily undertaken. At her maximum speed of 6.75 knots, she had an endurance of just over fourteen hours, which increased to twenty-four hours at her cruising speed. The crew of seven included a mechanic.

The decision to send one of the new Surf types to Wells was explained by Admiral of the Fleet Sir Henry Oliver in February 1935 when he visited the north Norfolk coast, while the stationing of a motor lifeboat at Wells meant the Brancaster and Blakeney lifeboats would be withdrawn. Indeed, by the time the new lifeboat arrived at Wells on 11 February 1936, both

The Surf motor lifeboat Royal Silver Jubilee 1910–1935 *was built in 1935 by Groves & Guttridge at Cowes, and was powered by two 12hp Weyburn F2 petrol engines driving two Hotchkiss Internal Cone propellers. (RNLI)*

Wells first motor lifeboat, the 32ft Surf type Royal Silver Jubilee 1910–1935 *on her launching carriage with the Case L launching tractor T32 (reg no.FYE 221) which was on station from July 1939 to 1954 and was the station's second tractor. (From an old postcard supplied by Allen Frary)*

Wells first motor lifeboat Royal Silver Jubilee 1910–1935 *on her carriage outside the lifeboat house prior to her naming ceremony on 13 July 1936 with F.T. Everard's sailing barge* Greenhithe *passing. She was christened by the donor Mrs E.W. Montford, patron of the Ladies' Lifeboat Guild at Stoke-on-Trent, who ended the formal ceremony by saying 'I name this lifeboat* Royal Silver Jubilee, 1910–1935, *and wish her crew every success'. (Wells History Society)*

The scene outside the lifeboat house during the naming of Wells' first motor lifeboat Royal Silver Jubilee 1910–1935, *with crowds of supporters many of whom had travelled from Stoke-on-Trent for the event. (Supplied by Paul Russell)*

Royal Silver Jubilee 1910–1935 *is launched across the beach watched by holiday-makers. (Wells History Society)*

these stations had been closed after sixty-one and seventy-three years' service respectively. The new boat, built by Groves & Guttridge at East Cowes, was funded from the gift of Mrs E.W. Montford, JP, of Market Drayton, Shropshire. Mrs Montford made the gift to commemorate the Silver Jubilee of King George V and the boat was thus named *Royal Silver Jubilee 1910–1935*. The lifeboat was taken by train to Wells, preceded by its carriage which was fitted with caterpillar wheels, and a caterpillar tractor was supplied for launching. The lifeboat was taken on a railway truck to the Custom House quay and, watched by a small crowd, lowered by crane into the water. Between 17 and 21 February, the Eastern District Inspector of Lifeboats Lieut Cdr P.E. Vaux took the lifeboat out on trials to familiarise the crew with the new craft which, with its engine, was significantly different from anything operated at the station hitherto.

The naming ceremony took place on 13 July 1936, and the Stoke-on-Trent branch, together with the Stoke-on-Trent and Newcastle-under-Lyme Ladies' Lifeboat Guilds, organised a trip to Wells for the event. About 150 came by special train, including the Lord Mayor and Lady Mayoress of Stoke, the Deputy Mayor of Newcastle, and officers of the branch and the two guilds. After the ceremony the party visited Sandringham where, though it was not a public day, they were shown over the gardens by special permission of the King. The Earl of Leicester, patron and president of the Wells branch, managed the proceedings. Mrs Montford presented the lifeboat to Sir Godfrey Baring, RNLI chairman, who paid a tribute to the lifeboatmen of Norfolk and then formally handed the lifeboat into the care of branch chairman F. Raven. The lifeboat was dedicated by the Revd F.G. Beddard, Rector of Wells, and a vote of thanks was proposed by Herbert Loynes, honorary secretary. The ceremony ended with Mrs Montford christening the lifeboat which was launched by tractor.

The first service performed by the new motor lifeboat took place on 26 March 1936 when she went to help survivors from the steamship *Boree*, of Caen, which had been in collision with the Spanish steamer *Aizkarai Mendi* off the East Dudgeon Lightvessel. *Aizkarai Mendi* did not need any help, but *Boree* foundered and, of twenty-two crew, thirteen were rescued by vessels in

Royal Silver Jubilee 1910–1935 *on service to the Dutch motor vessel* Karanan *in September 1936 with the tug* Scotsman *assisting in the rescue work. (Allen Frary collection)*

the area. When news of the collision reached shore, Cromer No.1 lifeboat *H.F. Bailey* and *Royal Silver Jubilee 1910–1935* were launched at 9 a.m. and 9.35 a.m. respectively. The Cromer boat took seven men from one of the vessels and searched for other survivors without success. She then returned to Wells with the Wells lifeboat as the poor weather meant she could not rehouse up the slipway at Cromer. *Royal Silver Jubilee 1910–1935* reached her station at 5.45 p.m. and the Cromer boat was piloted in by the Wells second coxswain and left at moorings.

Less than two months later, on 24 May 1936, *Royal Silver Jubilee 1910–1935* was again in action. At 7 a.m., the motor cruiser *Water Nymph* left Wells for Boston, with the second coxswain and another man on board. When they saw she was flying distress signals, the lifeboat launched at 9.15 a.m. into a moderate to strong breeze with a rough sea. The lifeboat found the cruiser about two miles north-north-west of the harbour with her engine broken, so the lifeboat towed her back to harbour and then returned to station.

The final service of 1936 was a rather long drawn-out affair that began on the night of 20 September after the motor vessel *Karanan*, of Rotterdam, from Groningen for King's Lynn, went ashore a mile east of Blakeney Point in a strong easterly wind with rough seas. *Royal Silver Jubilee 1910–1935* was launched at 10.35 p.m. and the Sheringham lifeboat *Foresters' Centenary* (ON.786) an hour later. Heavy seas broke over the Sheringham lifeboat as she was launched, washing her off the carriage, but she was got away with the help of the haul-off rope. Both lifeboats stood by the motor vessel, which had a crew of ten and a cargo of strawboards, throughout the night. At about 7 a.m., a tug arrived and a rope was passed to the steamer by the Wells lifeboat. At high water *Karanan* did not refloat, but was not in any immediate danger so the Sheringham lifeboat returned to station as did the Wells lifeboat. Sheringham lifeboat had been out for twelve hours, and the Wells boat for more than thirteen. Eight days later, on

29 September, tugs again tried to refloat *Karanan*. As a boat was needed for liaison work, and with the weather too bad for an ordinary boat, *Royal Silver Jubilee 1910–1935* launched to assist, with a squally north wind blowing and rough sea. The lifeboat was on service from 2.30 p.m. to 8.20 p.m. on 29 September, and again from 5 a.m. to 10.45 a.m. on 30 September. *Karanan* was eventually towed off and taken to King's Lynn.

The following year, 1937, proved to be a fairly busy one for the Wells lifeboat which completed four effective services. The first took place on 7 February after the local motor fishing boat *Liberty* was delayed in getting back to harbour by a fouled propeller. *Royal Silver Jubilee 1910–1935* launched at 4.20 p.m., met *Liberty* about three miles out, and escorted her in. The next service took place during the evening of 24 July after the motor yacht *Gazeka*, of London, came ashore at Blakeney Point with her engine disabled. *Royal Silver Jubilee 1910–1935* launched at 7.30 p.m. into a heavy thunderstorm, reached *Gazeka* just over an hour later, took her in tow, and brought her and the six people on board to Wells Harbour. On 19 November, the coastguard reported the auxiliary ketch *Elizabeth*, bound from Hamburg to Syria, ashore about two and a half miles east of the entrance to Wells Harbour. *Royal Silver Jubilee 1910–1935* launched at 10.45 a.m. and found the vessel, with her crew of four, high and dry. The lifeboat stood by all day, but no tug arrived, eventually the lifeboat went alongside *Elizabeth* and took off the four men and the dog. She landed them at Wells Quay and returned to station at 8.30 p.m. after having been on service for nearly ten hours. The final service of the year, on 8 December, saw *Royal Silver Jubilee 1910–1935* launching at low water, which involved being taken two miles on her carriage over the sands by the motor tractor, to the motor vessel *Helen Birch,* of Hull, which had a crew of four and was bound with a cargo of wheat for Wells. The lifeboat stood by in worsening conditions and then piloted the vessel into deep water so that a lifeboatman could be put on board. Eventually, *Helen Birch* was brought safely to harbour.

The motor vessel Karanan *stranded east of Blakeney Point before she was towed off, September 1936. Both Wells and Sheringham lifeboats attended the vessel over a period of several days. (Allen Frary collection)*

Royal Silver Jubilee 1910–1935 on service to the steamship Faxfleet, *of Goole, on 15 January 1941. The steamer had gone aground on the Haisborough Sands and had got off but was leaking so badly that her master had beached her at Stiffkey to save her from sinking. The lifeboat stood by and took off seven of her crew of sixteen and landed them at the boathouse, returning to stand by until after high water. (From a painting by Mick Bensley)*

On 22 July 1939, a new Case 'Roadless' type L launching tractor, number T32, arrived at the station to replace the 1927-built Clayton & Shuttleworth vehicle, number T19, that had been supplied in February 1936 when the motor lifeboat had first arrived. The new tractor, which was 15ft in length, had a width of 6ft 6in, and a height of 8ft, weighed six and a half tons and was more powerful than the tractor it replaced. It was housed in the lifeboat house, but a tractor garage with a concrete ramp and separate entrance, built on the south end of the lifeboat house, was completed in May 1940. This tractor served until the mid-1950s and made the task of launching and recovering the lifeboat, a difficult one particularly at low tide, considerably easier for the shore crew.

The Second World War proved to be a busy time for *Royal Silver Jubilee 1910–1935.* East Anglia was often in the front line of battle as aircraft from both sides criss-crossed the area making casualties at sea inevitable and the Wells lifeboat was regularly called upon. The first wartime service, on 23 December 1939, was a routine affair after three fishing boats were reported overdue. Two had come back at about 11 a.m. but the third, *Malvina,* with a crew of three, was missing. *Royal Silver Jubilee 1910–1935* launched at 3.30 p.m., found *Malvina* to the east of Wells Harbour, and escorted her in. Another straightforward service was performed on 1 March 1940 after a ship's boat was reported adrift about two miles off. In moderate conditions, *Royal Silver Jubilee 1910–1935* launched at 1.15 p.m. and found the boat with no one on board. It belonged to the French steamer *P.L.M. 25,* of Rouen, which had been sunk as a result of enemy action. Four of the steamer's crew lost their lives, but the remaining twenty-seven were saved by a British warship. The boat was towed back to Wells by the lifeboat.

Just over a month after this last service, *Royal Silver Jubilee 1910–1935* was taken to Oulton Broad for a complete overhaul on 9 April 1940 during which time Wells was without a lifeboat. She returned on 18 August but a few days later was placed off service again after one of her gear pistons had broken. This was repaired but not until 8 November was she back on service, after an overhaul of her gearbox, which was followed by an exercise launch to ensure she was fully operational.

During 1941, *Royal Silver Jubilee 1910–1935* performed three services, two of which involving crashed aeroplanes. The first was on 6 May 1941 when she launched at 6.30 p.m. to the steamship *Radstock*, of Bridgwater, a mile north of Wells Bar. Bound from Avonmouth for Wells, the steamer was short of water, coal and food, her degaussing gear was broken and she could not get a pilot. The lifeboat assisted by landing the captain and putting a pilot on board. On 26 June, the RAF reported an aeroplane crashed in the sea so *Royal Silver Jubilee 1910–1935* launched at 9.45 a.m. to search for it. About five miles from the boathouse, a rubber balloon was spotted, but nothing else was found despite a thorough search of the area. The final service of the year was on 27 November when *Royal Silver Jubilee 1910–1935* was launched after an aeroplane had been reported down in the sea. The winding channel to the sea full of shoals was made more difficult to negotiate as wartime blackout regulations meant no lights were shown. On her way down the channel, the lifeboat found an RAF rescue launch, which was also going out, in difficulties. Coxswain Theodore Nielsen put the second coxswain on board the launch to pilot her, and the honorary secretary Dr E. W. Hicks also went on board. The launch then went to sea followed by the lifeboat. When the launch was near to the position given by the coastguard, her lamp was flashed and at once a small answering light appeared. The launch was guided to a rubber dinghy in which were six airmen, the crew of a Wellington bomber. The launch rescued them, took the

Royal Silver Jubilee 1910–1935 alongside the Lancaster bomber on 14 July 1942. Coxswain Theodore Neilsen walked along the wing of the crashed plane, endagering his own life, to check whether any survivors remained inside the fuselage. (From a painting by Mick Bensley)

Coxswain Theodore Neilsen (centre in dark cap) with Wells lifeboat crew in front of Royal Silver Jubilee 1910–1935, *possibly during the boat's naming ceremony. The crew are, left to right, George Fuller, Alf Powditch, Rolly Grimes, Sam Abel, Billy Cox, Neilsen, Jimmy Cox (Mechanic) and Loady Cox. (Courtesy of Wells Lifeboat Station)*

dinghy in tow, and the second coxswain of the lifeboat piloted her up the channel again. The lifeboat saw her returning so turned back herself.

On 9 January 1942, the services of the Wells lifeboat were requested late in the afternoon after a tug showing flares off Scolt Head had been seen. As the tide was low, *Royal Silver Jubilee 1910–1935* had to be taken three miles across the sand before she could be launched, putting out into rough seas and snow squalls. She found nothing at the position given, but lights were seen a long way off in the same direction. The collier *Eastwood*, of London, was found at anchor and leaking, and her master asked the lifeboat to assist. So *Royal Silver Jubilee 1910–1935* stood by until a tug arrived to take the steamer in tow, and then returned to her station at 3.25 a.m. on 10 January. The tug that had been seen off Scolt Head, and to which the lifeboat had originally launched, was aided by the Skegness lifeboat *Anne Allen* (ON.760).

The other service performed by the Wells lifeboat in 1942 began at 5.39 a.m. on 14 July after a message was received that a Lancaster bomber aeroplane had ditched in the sea three miles away. *Royal Silver Jubilee 1910–1935* was launched at 6.15 a.m. with honorary secretary Dr E.W. Hicks on board and found the aeroplane standing on her nose, with her tail and part of her port wing blown away. One airman, in a weak state but still conscious, moaning with pain and clinging to the underside of the port wing, was lifted into the lifeboat. As no sign of any other member of the crew could be seen, Coxswain Theodore Neilsen hoisted himself on to the edge of the wing and walked along to the fuselage. Its top had been blown away and he climbed inside to search for the rest of the crew, who might still be aboard, injured and helpless. At any moment the aeroplane could have turned over or sunk, trapping the coxswain inside. Fortunately this did not happen and, as the search proved fruitless, Neilsen climbed back aboard the lifeboat which returned to Wells. The injured man was taken to hospital, but he later died. The lifeboat went back to the aeroplane and made a further search, but found nothing except a rubber dinghy about a mile away. Although the aeroplane sank, an Air–Sea Rescue launch with other aeroplanes made a wider search and the lifeboat returned to station. Some of the bodies of the other six airmen from the bomber were eventually recovered. In recognition of his gallantry in going on board the aeroplane, the Thanks Inscribed on Vellum was accorded to Coxswain Neilsen.

To assist in saving ditched air crews, an airborne lifeboat was developed by Uffa Fox. It could be carried under a specially adapted aircraft and dropped by parachute to survivors adrift in rubber dinghies. The airborne lifeboats were fitted with small petrol engines and sails for propulsion, and carried a radio and supplies. On 5 May 1943, an airborne lifeboat was used in rescue work for the first time when one was dropped to a ditched crew in the North Sea somewhere off the Norfolk coast. The boat's motor broke down, however, when it was about twelve miles from Wells and so *Royal Silver Jubilee 1910–1935* was launched to assist. But the faster Air–Sea Rescue launch, also based at Wells, got to the boat first and the lifeboat was not needed.

Services during 1944 were all to wartime vessels. On 10 January 1944, *Royal Silver Jubilee 1910–1935* launched to the Admiralty Drifter No.634, with a crew of five aboard, which had broken down at the entrance to Wells Harbour. The drifter was dragging her anchor just clear of the bar so a member of the lifeboat crew went aboard to act as a pilot and, with the lifeboat's help, she reached Wells Harbour. On 3 November the naval authorities at Great Yarmouth reported

An old postcard entitled 'The Wells Motor Lifeboat' showing Royal Silver Jubilee 1910–1935 *emerging from the boathouse on her carriage. The Clayton tractor on the right, T19 built in 1927, was the first tractor to serve at Wells.*

Wells lifeboat crew in front of Royal Silver Jubilee 1910–1935. *From left to right: Alf Powditch, Sam Abel, George Fuller, Titch Pegg, Billy Cox, Herbert Coe, Coxswain Theodore Neilsen (in dark cap), Reggie Grimes, Jimmy Cox, Charlie Stevenson, Cyril Grimes, Frank Taylor and Ernie Jarvis. (Wells History Society)*

that a motor vessel, outside Wells Harbour, was leaking and in need of help. *Royal Silver Jubilee 1910–1935* was launched and found the War Department motor vessel *Caddel* with a crew of five. Two lifeboatmen went aboard the vessel which was then brought in.

Ten days later, on 13 November, *Royal Silver Jubilee 1910–1935* was again called into action for what proved to be an arduous service. A landing craft got into difficulties outside Wells Harbour in a strong north-west wind and rough seas. The lifeboat put out at 6.10 p.m. and, despite rain and darkness, the lifeboatmen found the vessel *LCT 908* ashore on the east side of the harbour. As the sea was too rough to approach the vessel from outside the harbour, the lifeboat re-entered the harbour and got close from that direction. But when the lifeboat's anchor was let go, it fouled and she was grounded. As it was low water, the lifeboat crew laid out both their own anchor and that of the landing craft to await the tide turning. When the tide made and the lifeboat floated, she was positioned inside the harbour showing a light to guide the vessel if she refloated, but she remained stuck on the bank. The lifeboat stood by until after high water and then returned to station, arriving at 8 a.m. on 14 November having been out for fourteen hours. Because they had been out all night in bad weather, the crew received increased monetary awards.

This proved to be the last rescue undertaken by *Royal Silver Jubilee 1910–1935* which, in 1945, was replaced by a new motor lifeboat, although her life-saving days were not over. In June 1946 she was given to the Royal North and South Netherlands Lifeboat Society, the KNZHRM, whose fleet had been decimated by the actions of the occupying Nazi forces during the Second World War. Renamed *Rosilee*, she served at the Vlieland station from 1946 until 1959 proving to be an ideal design for the shallow beaches of the Dutch coast. She was sold by the KNZHRM in 1959 since when her whereabouts are unknown.

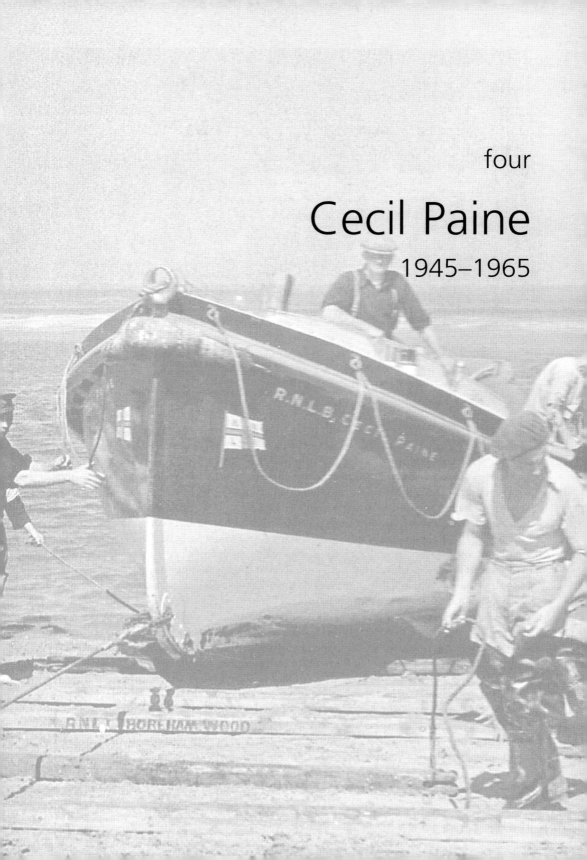

four

Cecil Paine

1945–1965

At the end of the Second World War, Wells was one of the first stations to receive a new lifeboat. In November 1941, the district inspector had told the local branch that a larger lifeboat would be supplied 'when conditions permitted' and as soon as the war was over a new boat, ON.850, was allocated to the station. The boat was the first of a new class of twin-engined 35ft 6in Liverpool motor lifeboats to be built. This type of non-self-righting lifeboat had previously been built with only a single engine. The new boat was more powerful than the 32ft Surf type, being fitted with twin 18bhp Weyburn AE.4 petrol engines that gave her a top speed of 7.42 knots and a cruising speed of seven knots. Although the prototype of the twin-engined Liverpool class had been laid down in 1940, it was destroyed in an aid raid on the boatyard and so the Wells boat was the first of the new class. The Liverpool was intended for stations that employed carriage launching and was the heaviest carriage lifeboat built to date. The development of the motor tractor during the inter-war years, when its use became widespread, meant that weight was not such a major consideration when designing a carriage boat and ON.850 weighed almost eight tons. Built by Groves & Guttridge at a cost of £7,462, she was provided from the legacy of Mr A.C. Paine and named *Cecil Paine*. After trials, the new lifeboat was placed on station at Wells on 25 July 1945.

Within six months of *Cecil Paine* being placed on station, an unusual attempt was made to steal her. During the night of 7 January 1946, six German prisoners of war, who were waiting to be repatriated in the aftermath of the conflict, escaped from Matlaske POW camp, stole a lorry and drove to the lifeboat house. A local garage man, Mr S. Abel, saw the lorry go down Beach Road without lights and so telephoned the police, who rushed to the lifeboat house in time to catch the six men as they were leaving. The POWs had broken open a window of the house, removed the covers of the lifeboat and tried, unsuccessfully, to start its engine. The Germans must have realised that launching the boat undetected, when a tractor and shore helpers were needed, would be impossible and gave up. They were recaptured within an hour of their escape and the damage done to the lifeboat was made good.

The first service by the new lifeboat took place during February 1947 after a ship was seen anchored about two and a half miles north-east of the harbour in need of assistance. Just after midnight, the vessel requested the lifeboat stand by and so at 1.35 a.m. on 9 February *Cecil Paine* was launched into a strong easterly breeze and very rough sea. She found the motor vessel *Spirality*, of London, which was dragging her anchors despite having three down. The lifeboat stood by until a tug arrived at 6 a.m., took the motor vessel in tow, and made for King's Lynn. The lifeboat returned to her station, arriving at 8.30 a.m.

In 1947, Theodore Neilsen retired from the position of coxswain, having been one of very few foreign born men to be elected to such a position on a British lifeboat. He went to sea at the age of fourteen and first came to Wells in 1910 in a three-masted schooner. In 1914 he married the daughter of Charlie Wordingham, a Wells pilot, and soon joined the local fishermen to replace his brother-in-law, who had been called up for naval service. He became a member of the lifeboat crew in 1910, and was made bowman, second coxswain and then coxswain in 1933. During the Second World War, Neilsen lead flotillas of boats from Wells, Blakeney and Brancaster to help at Dunkirk, and was made an MBE for his efforts. After the end of the war,

The 35ft 6in Liverpool motor Cecil Paine was built by Groves & Guttridge, Cowes, and was one of the first lifeboats to be completed after the end of the Second World War. She served at Wells from 1945 to 1965 and saved twenty lives during that time. (Wells History Society)

The 1945-built Liverpool motor Cecil Paine being hauled back into the boathouse. (EDP, supplied by Paul Russell)

he was chosen to represent Norfolk fishermen in the Victory Parade in London. Neilsen died on 28 January 1961 and his ashes were scattered off the Wells coast from *Cecil Paine* after a service was held on the beach. The Rector of Wells, the Revd W. Alexander Stephens, conducted the service, and the lesson was read by Coxswain David Cox who had joined the crew in the 1940s and took over as coxswain in January 1960.

Cecil Paine's next service took place on 25 July 1948 after an explosion in the engine room of the Royal Fleet Auxiliary oil tanker *Wave Commander* had caused injuries to some of the tanker's crew. The ship was twenty miles north-east of Wells and a doctor was needed. The lifeboat launched into a moderate sea at 7 a.m. with honorary secretary Dr E.W. Hicks on board. The lifeboat reached the position given but, as the weather was hazy, nothing could be seen. The lifeboat crew got further information through the East Dudgeon Lightvessel and eventually found the ship. Dr Hicks went aboard to treat the injured men, one of whom was badly hurt. With some difficulty, he was lifted into the lifeboat on a stretcher and then landed at Holkham, where he had to be pushed on a hand cart over a mile of sands to a waiting ambulance, before the lifeboat returned to station.

During 1949, *Cecil Paine* undertook three services. On 28 January 1949, after the owner of the local motor fishing boat *Sally* reported she was overdue, the lifeboat launched at 4.55 p.m. to search. An hour later the lifeboat found the boat aground half a mile east-south-east of the harbour bar, refloated her and towed her in. At 10.30 p.m. on 16 July 1949, *Cecil Paine* launched, with the second coxswain in command, to the RASC motor vessel *Fagin*, with a crew of four, two miles north-west of the harbour. The skipper wanted to get to Wells but could not find the way. Two lifeboatmen boarded *Fagin* and she then made for Wells guided by the lifeboat. The final service of the year took place in the afternoon of 30 September 1949 after the coxswain

Cecil Paine *outside the lifeboat house during the scattering of ashes service for Coxswain Theodore Neilsen, 7 February 1961. (Courtesy of Wells Lifeboat Station)*

Cecil Paine stands by the steamship Zor, *on her way from Finland to Hull, in May 1955 with the steamer* Richmond Queen *standing by as wood from the casualty falls into the sea. (From a painting by Mick Bensley)*

realised that two fishing boats were still out and the weather had worsened. *Cecil Paine* launched at 1.32 p.m. into rough seas and found the local boats *Spero* and *Blanche* off the harbour bar, so escorted them in.

No services were undertaken in 1950 and only one in 1951, on 4 July, when nine local fishing boats were caught at sea in a gale and *Cecil Paine* escorted them to harbour. But on 30 January 1952, *Cecil Paine* and the Wells lifeboatmen were involved in a tragic incident when two fishermen lost their lives while out fishing about a mile from the bar. George Money, Raymond Money and Cyril Everitt, who were also lifeboatmen, were working the pots from their fishing boat *Tony* but were having difficulty with their gear. They were hauling whelk pots when one of the tows from the pots jammed between the rudder and the deadwood causing the boat to swing stern to tide. Ray Money and Cyril Everitt both climbed onto the aft locker and were trying to lift the rudder upwards to clear the rope when the tiller swung round and knocked both overboard. They had lifted the rudder off the bottom pin rendering the boat rudderless. With both men in the water and the boat now free of the rope but with no serviceable steering, George Money threw an oar into the water hoping that the men would cling to it, but unfortunately neither reached it. Crews on the other fishing boats immediately went to help but found no trace of the men in spite of a one and a half hour search which was only abandoned at darkness. The lifeboat was launched at 6.44 p.m. to cover the area using her searchlights in the dark and returned after three hours with some of the missing equipment, but no trace of the men.

On 18 May 1955, Wells lifeboat crew worked with the neighbouring crew from Sheringham on what proved to be a rather long drawn out service after Coxswain William Cox was informed by the coastguard that the steamship *Zor*, of Istanbul, was in difficulty six miles west-north-west of the Dudgeon Lightvessel. *Cecil Paine* was launched into a northerly gale accompanied by

Advances in life-saving equipment continued during the 1950s including development by the RNLI, in conjunction with the Fowler company, of a more powerful launching tractor. The Fowler Challenger tractor was introduced in 1953 with the first, T56, sent for service at Hoylake on the Wirral. Two further Challengers were built in 1953 with the next one, T59, sent to Wells in April 1954, as pictured above launching Cecil Paine. *Its arrival 'created considerable interest and [it] was inspected by a large crowd', according to the local newspaper account. The crowd remained in attendance to watch the launching trials involving the tractor conducted by personnel from the RNLI including Lieut Cdr E. W. Middleton, the RNLI's Inspector General, Lieut Cdr H. Harvey, district inspector for the Eastern area, B. Rickard, the district engineer, and Mr A. Curtis, the carriage surveyor. The lifeboat was taken from the lifeboat house by the old tractor so that the Challenger, which weighed twelve tons 18cwt 2qrs compared with approximately five tons of the vehicle it was replacing, would not damage the lifeboat house's foundations. The Challenger was then coupled to the lifeboat which it hauled over the beach for about two miles towards Holkham for a low water trial. Instructions were given to the crew by Fowler's representatives from Leeds. The new tractor was fitted with a 95hp Meadows DC630 diesel engine, had six forward and four reverse gears, and was waterproofed and capable of operating continuously at full power when in water several feet deep. It served at Wells until November 1969 and was subsequently stationed at Kilmore Quay and Newcastle. (EDP, courtesy of Paul Russell)*

squalls of sleet and reached *Zor* at 6.55 p.m. to find her anchored and listing about forty degrees to starboard. *Zor*, was loaded with timber and, as each successive sea hit her, the wood fell from her deck into the sea. The steamship *Richmond Queen* was standing by and had taken on board the wife of *Zor*'s captain and several members of the crew who had got clear in one of the boats. The captain of *Richmond Queen* asked the coxswain to run a line to *Zor* which he did by going along *Zor*'s port side and securing a rope aboard to keep the lifeboat in position, although at times the lifeboat was hitting *Zor*'s bilge keel. One of *Zor*'s crew slid down a rope into the lifeboat followed by the captain, who was taken to *Richmond Queen* so that he could talk to his wife and to *Richmond Queen*'s captain. After ten minutes, he asked the coxswain to put him back aboard his own ship, a feat that was only accomplished with considerable difficulty.

When some of *Zor*'s crew indicated they wished to leave her, the coxswain brought the lifeboat alongside once more and took off four men and some baggage. At the request of *Richmond Queen*'s captain, Coxswain Cox then took another line to *Zor* as the first had parted while again trying unsuccessfully to persuade the rest of the crew to abandon ship. As the lifeboat was by now running low on fuel, she left *Zor* in the early hours of 19 May to return to Wells, land the survivors and refuel, leaving Sheringham lifeboat *Foresters' Centenary* (ON.786) and the tug *Serviceman* on scene.

Sheringham lifeboat had reached *Zor* at 6 a.m. and found the casualty still lying at anchor with a heavy list to starboard, surrounded by timber which continued to be washed out as seas struck her. Coxswain Henry West approached *Zor* from astern and, after circling her, approached her starboard side through a gap in the floating timber. He asked the captain to abandon ship, but the captain refused so the coxswain then made for the tug to discover that an attempt to tow would be made as soon as the weather moderated. The lifeboat stood by until 8.30 a.m., when the tug managed to get a line aboard but, by then, as *Zor* listed even further, the captain had decided to abandon ship. Due to the floating timber, Coxswain West had to risk taking the crew off on the weather side. After a rope had been passed between the two vessels, the captain and the three remaining members of the crew slid down the rope onto the deck of the lifeboat. Soon afterwards *Zor* slowly began to sink stern first. For this service in which two Norfolk lifeboats had played their part, the Thanks of the Institution on Vellum was accorded to both Coxswain Cox, of Wells, and Coxswain West, of Sheringham.

During 1956, services of a more routine nature were undertaken. On 22 March 1956, *Cecil Paine* launched after the second coxswain had received a report that the local motor fishing boat *Harvester*, of Wells, was overdue. The lifeboat found *Harvester* and her two-man crew two miles north-west of the harbour with a broken down engine, so towed her to Wells. On 28 May, *Cecil Paine* launched at 10 p.m. to the yacht *Wire*, of Glasgow, with one person on board, which was in difficulties a mile and a half east–north-east of Wells bar. The yacht's mainsail was damaged

The plaque displayed in the boathouse on which the inscription reads 'in recognition and appreciation of sea search operations for missing B-66 Aircraft, October 1961'. It was presented to the station at the RAF Base Sculthorpe by the 47th Bombardment Wing USAF. A dinner was held at the base for not only Wells lifeboat crew but all lifeboat crews from Skegness to Lowestoft. Apparently there was an un-named VIP aboard the plane at the time of the crash.
(Nicholas Leach)

Coxswain David Cox, right, on the beach while reserve lifeboat Lucy Lavers *is recovered in the background. Cox, who joined the crew in the 1940s, took over as coxswain from his Uncle Billy Cox on 1 January 1960. He retired on 14 August 1987 having held no other position other than crew member before being voted as coxswain. He remained a retained coxswain throughout this period whilst working as a whelk fisherman within the family business. He was awarded the BEM in the 1982 New Year's Honour's List. (EDP, supplied by Paul Russell)*

and her auxiliary engine had broken down, so the lifeboat brought her into harbour just before midnight.

On 31 October 1956, *Cecil Paine* was involved in assisting the Sheringham lifeboat *Foresters' Centenary* during a long service to the steamship *Wimbledon*, which was in difficulty thirteen miles north of Cromer light. After launching, *Foresters' Centenary* took off eight men in seas 15ft in height which were sweeping over *Wimbledon's* foredeck. These men were then transferred to another ship, which was standing by a mile and a half away, to make it easier to take on board the remaining members of the *Wimbledon's* crew if they needed to be rescued. Coxswain Henry West, in command of the Sheringham lifeboat, decided he must continue to stand by *Wimbledon* and so requested Wells lifeboat launch and land the doctor and the master's dead body as well as bring more petrol for the his own boat. *Cecil Paine* put out at 11.30 a.m. and two and a half hours later had taken off the doctor and the dead body and transferred petrol to the Sheringham lifeboat before returning to her station. As *Wimbledon* was sinking and the situation was worsening, the remainder of the crew then decided to be taken off. So the Sheringham lifeboat was taken alongside four times to rescue five more men leaving three on board. In extremely confused seas and with *Wimbledon* sinking fast, coxswain and mechanic worked together to get the lifeboat into position to successfully rescue the remaining men. With the survivors on board, the coxswain made for Wells instead of risking the bad beaching conditions at Sheringham with

Cecil Paine *leaving Lowestoft Harbour after completion of an overhaul at Fletcher's yard where she went twice during the 1960s. (Courtesy of RNLI)*

Cecil Paine *at Lowestoft during one of her refits at Fletcher's yard. (Courtesy of the Port of Lowestoft Research Society)*

Cecil Paine launching to escort *Foresters' Centenary* into harbour. Three-quarters of an hour earlier *Wimbledon* had sunk. Sheringham Coxswain H.E.West was awarded the silver medal for gallantry and Mechanic E.C. Craske received the bronze medal for what had been an excellent service in which the Wells lifeboatmen had also played their part.

On 5 June 1957, *Cecil Paine* was launched at 11.15 a.m. into a rough sea to the converted ship's boat *Sailfish*, with one person on board, which had gone ashore on the east side of the bar. The lifeboat towed the casualty into harbour through heavy surf and returned to station at 1.30 p.m. After this routine service, *Cecil Paine* did not perform another effective service for more than four years. On 14 July 1961, she launched to the converted ship's boat *Boy John*, which was in difficulty about four miles north of Scott Head with a broken water pump. The second coxswain went on board the casualty, which had a crew of two, to assist and the lifeboat towed the boat to Wells. On reaching the bar the coxswain waited until the flood tide and then made for Wells Quay taking the lifeboat back to station at 6.45 a.m. after she had been out all night.

Between June and October 1962, the reserve lifeboat *Lucy Lavers* (ON.832), a single-engined 35ft 6in Liverpool motor built in 1939 for the Aldeburgh No.2 station, was at Wells while *Cecil Paine* went for overhaul at Fletcher's Boatyard, Lowestoft. The reserve lifeboat was launched six times during her stint but only performed one effective service, on 19 September, when she assisted the motor cruiser Y811 which was being towed to harbour by a sprat boat in rough seas. When the tow rope parted, *Lucy Lavers* was launched and found the cruiser anchored in broken, confused seas just inside the outer bar. The lifeboat went alongside, and a helicopter also arrived on scene, taking off one of the cruiser's two crew and landing him on the beach before returning for the other man. In the meantime the lifeboat crew had been trying to take the cruiser in tow. The helicopter took the second man off so two lifeboatmen went aboard Y811 and secured a tow rope enabling the cruiser to be towed to Wells.

After returning from overhaul in October 1962, *Cecil Paine* had to wait until May 1963 before performing her next service, but this proved to be a particularly notable one. Late in the evening of 18 May 1963, the cabin cruiser *Seamu*, of Frinton, with a crew of two, ran aground at the entrance to Blakeney Harbour. *Cecil Paine* was launched at 10.05 p.m. after the tractor and carriage had negotiated deep water to reach a suitable launching site. Second Coxswain Frank Taylor was in charge and honorary secretary, Dr E.W. Hicks, was also on board. The lifeboat reached the casualty within forty-five minutes and found it had let go an anchor which had fouled, making the boat lie with her stern to the seas which were breaking on board and gradually filling her. In her first approach to *Seamu*, the lifeboat touched bottom on a sandbank before she could get close enough to render assistance. Second Coxswain Taylor then took the lifeboat round the sandbank and anchored about 200 yards from *Seamu*. At 11 p.m., with sufficient water on the sandbank for the lifeboat to cross it, Taylor took his boat to within 100 yards upwind of the casualty and let go his anchor. With the wind increasing to near gale force, the lifeboat was veered down on her cable towards the cruiser and, after four attempts, she managed to get alongside. In the few moments their boat was next to the casualty, the lifeboatmen pulled the cruiser's crew of two off and to safety. The lifeboat was damaged as she was bumped against the cruiser's quarter during this procedure, but she safely got clear afterwards. The cruiser was then driven ashore and so, with no hope of saving it, Taylor sailed for the lifeboat station where *Cecil Paine* arrived at 3.15 a.m. on 19 May. For this outstanding service, undertaken in hazardous conditions, the bronze medal was awarded to Second Coxswain Taylor and medal service certificates issued to the honorary secretary and to Bowman John Cox, Mechanic James Cox, Assistant Mechanic Alan Cox and to Ronnie Taylor, Barry Leggatt and Alan Cooper.

Between 14 July 1963 and 27 April 1964, the reserve lifeboat *Lucy Lavers* was again on station while *Cecil Paine* was taken to Fletcher's Boatyard at Lowestoft to be re-engined with

Recovery of Cecil Paine *on the beach outside the lifeboat house using the Fowler Challenger tractor T59 (reg. no. OJJ 866) which served at Wells from 1954 to November 1969. (Courtesy of Fred Painter)*

Cecil Paine *being hauled onto her carriage during recovery watched by holiday-makers with Coxswain Ted Neilsen on right and head launcher Sid 'Crutchie' Smith on left. (Courtesy of Wells Lifeboat Station)*

new 32hp Parsons Penguin diesel engines. The reserve boat performed three services while at Wells, the first on 15 July 1963 when she landed three from a catamaran that was in tow of a fishing boat. She was called out again on 21 November, and found four sprat boats, west of the harbour, heavily loaded with fish. The lifeboat escorted them into harbour as they had difficulty in establishing their position in the driving spray and foam. The last service by *Lucy Lavers* took place during the morning of 9 February 1964 after the motor barge *Una* had grounded on the west side of Blakeney Harbour. Although the barge was in no immediate danger, her master asked the lifeboat to stand by when the tide flooded. When the barge's engine failed as she tried to pull herself clear, a line was made fast from *Lucy Lavers*. The barge was then towed clear by the lifeboat, safely moored in Blakeney Pit, and the lifeboat returned to station.

Cecil Paine returned in April 1964 and on 2 July was launched to a local fishing boat that was three hours overdue. After searching for nearly an hour and a half, the lifeboat found the fishing boat *Blanche* about three miles east of Blakeney Overfalls. Her engine had failed so she was towed back to Wells with her crew of three. On 19 August 1964, *Cecil Paine* was called out to the same fishing boat which, with two other fishing boats, *Sally* and *William Edward*, was making very heavy weather near Blakeney Overfalls. In gale-force winds, very rough seas and poor visibility, the lifeboat made for Blakeney Point where *Blanche* was found and escorted to Wells Harbour. The lifeboat then headed back to Blakeney Overfalls, found the other fishing boats and escorted *Sally* to Wells before returning to station.

What proved to be the final service performed by *Cecil Paine* during her time at Wells took place on 29 August 1964 and turned out to be a fine rescue. She was launched at 8.45 p.m. under the command of Coxswain David Cox after a yacht was seen burning a red flare half a mile west of Blakeney Harbour. Half an hour later the small auxiliary sloop *Kiskadee* was seen aground on a sandbank about half a mile west of Blakeney Point, lying beam to in confused seas. Coxswain Cox decided to anchor the lifeboat and veer down on to the yacht but, even with the full length of the anchor cable paid out, the lifeboat was unable to get close enough to the casualty. The anchor was hove up, a second attempt, also unsuccessful, was made to reach the yacht, while the third attempt resulted in the lifeboat hitting the bottom. A parachute flare showed that the yacht had, by now, been washed over a sand bar by the tide into comparatively smooth water and she was then in no immediate danger. When the tide rose, the lifeboat came off the bank and made a fourth attempt to reach the yacht. She was operating in heavy breaking surf which was continually sweeping over her and, once again, was unable to reach the yacht. Meanwhile another boat manned by S. Long, a member of the inshore rescue scheme, had also put out and in his boat succeeded in taking *Kiskadee* in tow. The lifeboat stood by while this was being done and then returned to station at 2.30 a.m. on 30 August. For their efforts during this difficult service, the Thanks on Vellum was accorded to Coxswain David Cox, and Vellum Service Certificates were issued to the crew, Acting Second Coxswain John Cox, Acting Bowman A. Warner, Mechanic Albert Court, Assistant Mechanic Alan Cox and crew members David Case and A. Fulford.

In June 1965, *Cecil Paine* was replaced by a new lifeboat and she left Wells for the last time in early July. She was taken to Tyrell's Yard, Arklow, for overhaul and survey and in October placed on station at Kilmore Quay in south-east Ireland. She served there until February 1972, launching on service twenty-two times, and in July 1973 was sold out of service. She was acquired by the Portuguese Lifeboat Society for £4,300 and, renamed *Patreo-Joao-Rangel*, continued her life-saving career in Portugal. She has recently been retired from life-saving duties but remains in Portugal.

Before *Cecil Paine* left, she was joined by an inshore rescue boat to supplement the life-saving capabilities of the station. The small inflatable rubber craft, costing £280, powered by a 40hp outboard motor, first arrived at Wells on 14 June 1963 to become only the third such craft to enter service with the RNLI after similar boats had been sent to Gorleston and Aberystwyth. The boat was second-hand and was used for crew training until the station's own boat, painted black and orange with 'RNLI Rescue' on the sides, arrived two weeks later.

The inshore rescue boats (IRBs), later designated inshore lifeboats (ILBs), were introduced by the RNLI in response to the increasing number of inshore incidents to which lifeboats were called. The growth of the leisure industry resulted in more people getting into difficulty, often within sight of the land and in moderate weather. Conventional lifeboats were not well suited to dealing with such incidents so the fast rescue craft was introduced to respond speedily and with a small crew. The RNLI bought an inflatable boat in 1962 for extensive trials, and a delegation visited France where similar boats were in operation to see the boats in service. Following these initial steps, the first IRBs were introduced during the summer of 1963. Such was their success that more and more places began to operate the boats in subsequent years. The 16ft inflatable

Coxswain David Cox (on right) and crew member A. 'Sonnie' Warner sitting on the IRB outside the small boathouse that was built for the craft adjacent to the offshore lifeboat's house. (EDP, supplied by Paul Russell)

The lifeboat house as it was in the 1960s with the small boathouse for the IRB alongside. In January 1978, the boathouse doors were damaged by severe storms while the IRB house was totally destroyed. (Courtesy of the RNLI)

lifeboats, made from tough nylon with neoprene, could be launched quickly and easily. Their speed of twenty knots was faster than any lifeboat in service during the 1960s, and they could easily go alongside other craft or persons in the water without causing or suffering damage.

Wells was chosen to receive one of the first of the new craft because the boat was ideally suited to the Norfolk coastline with its narrow creeks, sandbanks and shallow water. As soon as it arrived at the station, its capabilities were shown to local people and the press when two men were transferred without trouble from the lifeboat to the IRB, with one lifeboatmen commenting 'it's a bumpy ride but she's a lovely little boat'. To accommodate the IRB, a small house was built on the west side of the main boathouse and the boat was launched using a small trolley manhandled across the beach.

The new IRB, No. 11, was removed at the end of the summer season but returned in 1964 and was used for the first time on 1 May that year when three men were saved from the 25ft yacht *Skate*. The vessel went ashore on the outer bar while sailing from Burnham Overy to Morston. Second Coxswain Frank Taylor, Barry Leggatt and Tony Fulford went out in the IRB in a force five westerly wind and rough sea and attempted to refloat the boat, which had been bought at Burnham Overy and was being taken to Morston when it got into difficulties.

five

Ernest Tom Neathercoat

1965–1990

In June 1965, a new lifeboat, *Ernest Tom Neathercoat* (ON.982), was sent to Wells. She was one of the Oakley class self-righters built during the 1960s. Designed by and named after the RNLI's consulting naval architect, Richard Oakley, the type was 37ft in length, had a beam of 11ft 6in, and was manned by a crew of seven or eight. Developed during the mid-1950s, it was the first lifeboat design to have a high degree of inherent stability and also self-right in the event of a capsize. Self-righting was achieved through an ingenious water ballast system which transferred 1.54 tons of water ballast into a righting tank on the port side to right the boat in the event of a capsize. During trials, righting took about six seconds from the overturned position to the boat being upright. The 37ft Oakley's hull was of wood and, with a displacement of twelve and a half tons, the boat was suitable for handling ashore and carriage launching over a beach. The Wells boat was fitted with twin Ford Parsons Porbeagle four-cylinder diesels of 52bhp which gave a maximum speed of approximately eight knots.

The new £34,000 lifeboat reached Wells on 29 June 1965 after a 220-mile passage from Littlehampton that took twenty-eight and a half hours at sea and involved overnight stops at Dover and Lowestoft. The journey had been undertaken by Coxswain David Cox, Mechanic Albert Court, RNLI District Engineer Peter Rakestrow, crew members Alan Cooper and Richard Abel, and Lt Cdr Bruce Cairns, the district inspector. On reaching Wells, *Ernest Tom Neathercoat* was escorted home by *Cecil Paine* and moored at the quay next to her predecessor before being taken out of the harbour and launched on exercise from the lifeboat house for the first time.

The new lifeboat was officially named and dedicated on 8 July, just over a week after she had arrived, by Princess Marina, Duchess of Kent, who came to Norfolk to christen the new Cromer No.2 lifeboat *William Henry and Mary King* (ON.980) the same day. Princess Marina flew by helicopter to Holkham Hall for lunch with Lord Leicester, president of the Wells branch, and Lady Leicester, before being driven to Wells for the ceremony. Hundreds of guests, local residents, holidaymakers and schoolchildren watched the ceremony during which *Ernest Tom Neathercoat* was delivered to the care of the Wells branch by Commander Grenfell and accepted by Dr E.W. Hicks, station honorary secretary. The Bishop of Norwich, Dr Lancelot Fleming, dedicated the boat, assisted by the Rector of Wells, the Revd W. Alexander Stephens, and the minister of Wells Methodist Church, the Revd Frank Longley. After naming the boat, Princess Marina pressed a button to break the traditional champagne bottle over the bows and the boat was launched into the harbour channel. In the boathouse afterwards, the lifeboatmen, shorehelpers and former lifeboatmen, including six members of the Cox family of whelkers who between them had given over 200 years service in Wells lifeboats, were presented to Princess Marina.

Ernest Tom Neathercoat gave excellent service at Wells for a quarter of a century, during which time the crew performed some remarkable services. When replaced in 1990, she had launched eighty-five times on service and saved sixteen lives. Her first service took place on 31 July 1965, when she launched at 9.30 p.m. to the yacht *Eljida*, of Hull, in need of assistance two miles north-west of Blakeney Point. The lifeboat crew found the yacht, with a crew of three, required a pilot, so the lifeboat towed the yacht to Wells Quay and returned to her station. The second was at the end of December 1965 to the oil rig *Sea Gem* which collapsed and sank in the North Sea

The 37ft Oakley Ernest Tom Neathercoat *on trials shortly after being completed by William Osborne's yard at Littlehampton. When built, she had an open aft cockpit and was not fitted with radar. (Courtesy of the RNLI)*

Ernest Tom Neathercoat *arrives at Wells Quay for the first time, on 29 June 1965, having been escorted in by* Cecil Paine, *which is moored alongside. (EDP, supplied by Paul Russell)*

On 29 June 1969, the station celebrated its centenary when a commemorative vellum was presented to the local branch by Captain Robert Ryder, of the RNLI management committee. In the first 100 years of the stations existence, its lifeboats were launched on service 180 times and credited with saving 118 lives. The IRB had been launched eighteen times and saved seven lives during its five years at the station. The vellum was received by Dr Ernest Hicks, who retired after twenty-eight years as secretary. The vellum recorded the RNLI's thanks to the station and its crew for 'devotion and courage and for maintaining the high traditions of the lifeboat service'. (EDP, supplied by Paul Russell)

with thirty-two crew on board. Lifeboats from the Humber, Cromer No.1, Skegness and Wells stations launched to help, and spent a total of 113 hours at sea but the lifeboat crews were unable to find any survivors. *Ernest Tom Neathercoat* launched at midnight on 28 December and stood by during salvage operations, returning to station at 8.30 p.m. after twenty-one hours on service.

The following year, *Ernest Tom Neathercoat* was involved in a fine service that resulted in a framed letter of commendation signed by the RNLI chairman, Captain the Hon V.M. Wyndham-Quin RN being sent to Coxswain David Cox and the crew. On 15 September 1966, the yacht *Kylin* went aground to the west of the approach channel to Wells Harbour with only the owner, a seventy-year-old man, and his dog aboard. The coxswain walked across the sands and advised him to abandon his boat, which was high and dry, but he refused. Realising that the yacht would start to float as soon as there was enough water in the channel, the coxswain decided it would be advisable to launch the lifeboat. At 3.45 p.m. the inshore rescue boat launched to stand by the yacht in case the yacht should get into difficulties, while the lifeboat put out at 4.35 p.m. She was taken through the channel entrance to approach the yacht from seaward, by which time the wind had risen to force nine from the north-west accompanied by squally showers. As the lifeboat approached the yacht, it was afloat with a small outboard motor running and the owner trying to keep her head to wind but making no headway. The lifeboat went alongside and her crew grabbed the owner, who was somewhat reluctant to leave, and pulled him aboard the lifeboat. The man expressed concern about his dog, and the Bowman,

Ernest Tom Neathercoat *approaching Wells Quay (above) and moored alongside (below) for the presentation of the Centenary Vellum on 29 June 1969. (EDP, supplied by Paul Russell)*

During the latter half of the 1960s, three different inshore lifeboats were on station – No.8, No.82 from 1966 to 1968 and No.25, pictured at Morston following the capsize in 1968, from 1968 to 1969. All performed fine work as the new craft proved its worth during the decade, with a service on 6 April 1967 typical of the tasks for which it was intended. Two men reported missing on marshes east of the lifeboat house were seen on the sandhills and, with an exceptional tide caused by the onshore gale, they could not have crossed the marshes until well after dark. The IRB was therefore launched into the north-westerly gale and brought the two men to safety. (Supplied by Paul Russell)

John Cox, jumped aboard with a line. The yacht was taken in tow and secured at Wells Quay at 5.45 p.m. The other crew members were Frank Taylor, John Cox, Albert Court, Alan MacDonald Cox, Albert Warner and B. Leggatt.

A series of inshore lifeboats was operated during the summer months in the 1960s. Between May and August 1965, IRB No.29 was on station and undertook three services, the first on 13 June and the last on 8 August while the IRB was on exercise in a moderate easterly breeze. A dinghy capsized in rough seas on the bar throwing its crew of two into the water. The IRB immediately went to the scene, picked them out of the water and towed the dinghy back to the lifeboat station. Because of the nature of their design, the small inflatables were more at risk than the conventional lifeboats, and in late August 1968 the Wells IRB was capsized on service after being hit by a freak wave off Morston. The boat had been called out after a dinghy with four men on board was reported missing, but the dinghy made its way safely to Wells as the IRB was on its way out. On board the IRB when it capsized were Dick Abel and Tony Fulford, neither of whom were injured. They were able to right the boat and then rowed ashore at Morston from where it returned to Wells by road. Abel later explained: 'A wave hit us broadside on. We did not have a chance to go straight into it. We saw it too late'.

The work of life-saving continued during the 1970s, as *Ernest Tom Neathercoat* undertook a number of routine services, mainly to fishing vessels, as well as some more testing ones. On 10 April 1972, she escorted the fishing boats *Elizabeth* and *William Edward* and less than a month later assisted the fishing boat *Sovereign*, of Brancaster. On 21 October 1973, she launched to the motor fishing vessel *Pilgrim* which was in tow of the tug *Superman* just over twenty miles from Wells. As the fishing vessel appeared to be breaking up, in force nine winds and very heavy seas, the lifeboat put out to help at 5.15 a.m. She encountered heavy seas over the harbour bar but proceeded at full speed to the casualty's position, reported to be three miles north-west of the Dudgeon Shoal Buoy. At 6.55 a.m., a Sea King helicopter took off from RAF Leconfield and at 7.43 a.m. the tug reported that the men had been winched off by helicopter. Three minutes later, the lifeboat was released from service and returned to station. She was landed on the beach after coming through heavy surf in Holkham Bay and was recovered onto her carriage at low water. In recognition of the efforts made by Coxswain David Cox during what proved to be an ineffective service, he was accorded the RNLI's Thanks on Vellum.

Another long service was undertaken on 3 September 1974 when *Ernest Tom Neathercoat* was launched at 6.56 a.m. into force nine winds and very rough seas to stand by the motor vessel *Nordenstedt* of Hamburg. During the passage to the casualty from East Docking to North Race, the lifeboat experienced very bad sea conditions. At 10.58 a.m., the vessel was reported to be just over twelve miles from the Inner Dowsing and the lifeboat crew located the casualty by DF

On 8 June 1972, an Atlantic 17 ILB was sent to Wells for three weeks of evaluation trials. The boat was a new type of ILB with a fixed wooden hull with sponsons. A three-week trial at the station enabled the crew to assess whether this type of boat was suitable for rescue work. As well as trials the boat was used for rescues with the present Wells inshore boat acting as standby. The Atlantic, numbered B-6, was 16ft 6in in length, 6ft 10in in beam with a draught of only 9.5in. She had an operational radius of almost forty miles, a 50hp outboard motor, VHF radio and a resuscitator. Honorary Secretary David Case wanted an Atlantic 17 for Wells as the standard ILB because the station 'has to be prepared to deal with casualties anywhere between Blakeney and Hunstanton, even into the Wash'. The new boat would have been able to cover the distances more quickly, while being easier to handle and provide better crew comfort. But the Atlantic 17 type was only used on a trial basis as a development of the design, the larger Atlantic 21, proved to be a more suitable rescue craft and was adopted by the RNLI instead. Wells never received an Atlantic for operational service, but one was sent to the neighbouring Hunstanton station in the early 1980s and became responsible for covering the Wash. (EDP, supplied by Paul Russell)

Ernest Tom Neathercoat *launching on exercise on 4 February 1974 with Fowler tractor T68 (reg no. YUV 742) providing the power. The tractor was at Wells from 1969 to May 1974. The canopy over the lifeboat's cockpit was added to the boat to offer a degree of crew protection. (EDP, supplied by Paul Russell)*

and a parachute flare fired by the vessel provided a visual sighting. At 11.56 a.m., the lifeboat was alongside the motor vessel which, as the captain explained, had problems with her engine so he was requesting an escort to the Humber. At 12.30 p.m., the Humber lifeboat was tasked to take over the escort and she reached the casualty two hours later, enabling *Ernest Tom Neathercoat* to return to station. She reached Wells after 7 p.m. after more than twelve hours on service.

Between November 1976 and September 1977, the relief lifeboat *Calouste Gulbenkian* was on station while *Ernest Tom Neathercoat* went to J.E. Fletcher's yard at Oulton Broad for her five-yearly refit. The relief lifeboat performed one service during her time at Wells, standing by the 32ft fishing vessel *John B* on 5 June 1977 in force five to six winds after the vessel had drifted into broken water off Warham Hole. The boat was flooded and the SAR helicopter, which had arrived on scene, lifted off the crew. During her refit, *Ernest Tom Neathercoat* was fitted with radar which proved useful when working in poor visibility and during searches.

Ernest Tom Neathercoat returned to station on 25 September 1977 and performed her next service on 11 November when she launched to the cabin cruiser *Niny II* which was adrift with a broken down engine seventeen miles north of Wells. The fishing vessel *Sleep Robber* took the casualty in tow and the lifeboat arrived at 2.49 p.m., escorting the vessels to Brancaster. On 5 July 1978, the lifeboat went to the fishing vessel *Amethyst* which had broken down on Wells bar in very rough seas and towed the vessel to the quay. The same vessel got into difficulty again on 31 January 1979 eighteen miles off Wells and was again towed in by the lifeboat.

Perhaps the most remarkable service performed by *Ernest Tom Neathercoat* took place on 15 February 1979 when she went to the aid of the cargo vessel *Savinesti*, of Romania. The ship, with twenty-eight people on board was reported in distress thirty-seven miles from Spurn Point

The Fowler tractor is moved into position and the winch wire attached to the stern of Ernest Tom Neathercoat *ready to pull the lifeboat onto her launching carriage during a recovery outside the boathouse. (Campbell MacCallum)*

Ernest Tom Neathercoat *is secured on her carriage after being pulled onto it by the tractor following an exercise launch in the 1970s. (Campbell MacCallum)*

Wells lifeboat crew celebrate the RNLI's 150th anniversary in 1974 with tankards produced by Holkham Potteries to mark the event. From left to right: Doris Abel, -?-, Nigel Money, Richard Seeley, Alan Cooper, Roger Bishop, George Jay, Alan Cox, George Reed, David Cox, -?-, Billy Scoles, Tony Jordan, Graham Walker, David Case, Sonnie Warner and John Nudds. (Courtesy of Wells Lifeboat Station)

dragging her anchor and with engine failure. Communication was made difficult because heavy snow had brought down telephone wires, but Yarmouth Coastguard, the divisional inspector of lifeboats and the stations concerned decided that Wells lifeboat should launch to try to reach the casualty which was in danger of grounding on Race Bank or Docking Shoal. Another distress call had come to the north which Humber lifeboat might have to answer and no other lifeboat in the area could launch.

The morning was heavily overcast with continuous snow blizzards and poor visibility. The wind was north-easterly, strong gale force nine to storm force ten when *Ernest Tom Neathercoat* was launched into Wells Harbour at 10.24 a.m. under the command of Coxswain David Cox. At the entrance to the bar she was hit by heavy rolling seas and the full force of the wind. Being continually hit and filled by the seas, she lost her radar, MF radio and echo sounder. By 11 a.m., Coxswain Cox realised that the lifeboat was labouring to clear the water she was shipping and had to reduce speed. Although this prevented the labouring, she was still filling and the crew had to remain in the after cockpit as the heavy breaking seas made the forward well untenable throughout the service.

As Bridlington lifeboat had managed to launch to the casualty to the north, the Humber lifeboat was available to come south and, at 11.24 a.m., after her crew had boarded with great difficulty, the 54ft Arun *City of Bradford IV* (ON.1052) slipped her moorings and set course to clear the river at seventeen knots. Visibility was reduced to less than seventy-five yards by the

In the early 1970s, inshore lifeboat numbers had the prefix D- added to them and so the new boat that arrived in March 1970 for the decade's first summer season was D-113. A 15ft 6in RFD PB16 type inflatable, she remained at the station until 1976. In May 1976, a Zodiac Mk.II type, D-246 Spirit of Rotary *(pictured), was sent to the station, funded by the Rotary Club of St Ives, Cambridgeshire, and she served until 1987. (Supplied by Paul Russell)*

D class inflatable D-246 Spirit of Rotary *alongside* Ernest Tom Neathercoat. *(Supplied by Paul Russell)*

Ernest Tom Neathercoat undergoing her five-yearly refit and being fitted with radar at J.E. Fletcher's yard at Oulton Broad, December 1976. which cost about £1,500 and was funded by two members of the Georgian branch of the RNLI from Buckingham who had raised £2,500 for the lifeboat service. The boat was also fitted with a water heater to provide hot drinks for survivors and crew. (EDP, supplied by Paul Russell)

blizzard and, with a temperature of minus four degrees centigrade, a 3in layer of ice formed on the boat and rails. Superintendent Coxswain Brian Bevan eased back so that the thick ice on the scanners could be chipped away before the lifeboat resumed cruising speed. On clearing the river, speed had to be reduced because of the severe buffeting and zero visibility. At 11.13 a.m., *Savinesti* informed the coastal tanker *Annuity*, standing by the casualty, that she had lost both anchors but had enough power to hold into the weather while the ferry *Norwave* was also in the vicinity ready to assist.

At 12.14 p.m., Wells lifeboat crew sighted a ship and by 1.07 p.m. *Ernest Tom Neathercoat* was standing by *Savinesti*. Coxswain Cox asked if he could be relieved by Humber's Arun lifeboat as soon as possible as his crew were extremely cold in the open lifeboat. But for the next two hours, Wells lifeboat continued to stand by the casualty which held its own against the weather just north of South Race Buoy. The wind throughout was storm- to violent storm-force ten to eleven, accompanied by very heavy swell with 40ft breaking seas. Continuous heavy snow and spray reduced visibility to nil and at times all that could be seen of the other vessels by the lifeboat were the tips of their masts. Several attempts were made by *Annuity* and *Norwave* to pass a tow line to the casualty, but it could not be done. Meanwhile the tug *Lady Moira* and Humber lifeboat were both on their way, with the lifeboat stopping occasionally to chip ice off its fittings. At 3 p.m., when Humber lifeboat was seven miles away, Wells lifeboat was released to try to make the Norfolk coast in daylight. After *Ernest Tom Neathercoat* had departed, further unsuccessful attempts were made to establish a tow, but by the evening *Savinesti* was making four knots northwards under her own power. Running before the sea into the Humber, escorted by *Norwave* and *Lady Moira*, she managed to enter the safety of the river at 3.03 a.m.

Meanwhile, with the wind now violent storm-force eleven gusting to hurricane-force twelve, Wells lifeboat set course to South East Docking Buoy and, with her drogue streamed, started the return trip. It was soon found that the only course she could sustain without violent movement was south-west and she was held down to about half speed. The snow was blowing directly into the after cockpit and one crew member's task was to keep the screen and compass glass clear. At 6.15 p.m., the lifeboat crew glimpsed shore lights and an auxiliary coastguard ashore confirmed the lifeboat's position north of Brancaster Golf Club. An easterly course was then set for Wells Harbour. The remaining seven miles took two hours with frequent use of the helm and engines to bring the lifeboat into the breaking seas. At 8.26 p.m. the lifeboat was just west of Wells Bar but no leading lights could be seen through the blizzard so the local fishing boat *Strandline* came down the channel to act as a leading light and give pilotage. At 9.10 p.m., with her drogue out to its full extent, the lifeboat crossed the bar being completely swept by three seas as she came in. As the lifeboat could not be rehoused, she moored in the harbour at 9.50 p.m. with the crew being helped ashore as most were unable to walk due to the cold. They were helped into a change of clothes and driven to their homes. In all, *Ernest Tom Neathercoat*, an open 37ft lifeboat, was at sea for almost eleven and a half hours in violent storm conditions with very heavy swell and phenomenal seas frequently washing right over her, in a continuous blizzard, poor visibility and sub-zero temperatures. The snow was so bad that Wells was cut off for the following three days.

The crew from the Savinesti *service on board* Ernest Tom Neathercoat: *from left to right, David Cox, Tony Jordan, John Nudds, John Betts, Sonnie Warner, Albert Court, Graham Walker and Alan Cox.*

Ernest Tom Neathercoat *on service to the tug* Dockman *on 11 April 1983 with the motor fishing vessel* Isabel Deborah *escorting them into Brancaster. (From a painting by Mick Bensley)*

The lifeboat crew involved in the rescue of the tug Dockman *on 11 April 1983, from left to right: Allen Frary, Alan Cox, Tony Jordan (second coxswain), David Cox (coxswain), Auxiliary Coastguard Terry Scott, tug crewman, Fred Whitaker, tug crewman, Sonnie Warner, Graham Walker and John Betts.*

'The Rescue Team', a photograph taken in 1979, was originally intended only for display in the crew room and depicted lifeboat crew, officials, supporters, fund-raisers and the local coastguards as well as Ernest Tom Neathercoat and the ILB. The RNLI subsequently requested that they use it on a poster entitled 'Portrait of a Lifeboat Station'. It was distributed to all RNLI stations, branches, guilds and many organisations worldwide giving the station considerable publicity. Further such photos were produced in 1993 and again in 2000 for the 'Millennium Rescue Team' poster. (Campbell MacCallum)

For this extraordinary service, the silver medal was awarded to Coxswain Cox while the bronze medal went to Superintendent Coxswain Bevan of Humber lifeboat. Medal service certificates were presented to Second Coxswain Anthony Jordan, Mechanic Albert Court, Assistant Mechanic Alan Cox and crew members Albert Warner, John Nudds, Graham Walker and John Betts. The Humber lifeboat crew also received medal service certificates and framed letters of thanks signed by Major-General Ralph Farrant, chairman of the RNLI, were sent to the master of *Norwave*, Captain Wally Patch, and to the skipper of *Strandline*, John Ward.

Following three routine services in 1980, another excellent service was performed on 20 November 1981. At 2.25 p.m., the coastguard asked the lifeboat to launch to a possible casualty two and a half miles north of Brancaster and within fifteen minutes *Ernest Tom Neathercoat* was afloat under the command of Coxswain David Cox. With moderate visibility and a gale-force eight blowing, the lifeboat cleared the bar and turned west, leaving the rough seas and heavy swell on her starboard bow as she set out at full speed. At 3.10 p.m., an RAF Sea King helicopter reached the casualty, the fishing vessel *Sarah K*, whose engine room was flooded. Meanwhile, the lifeboat continued on her course until reaching the fishing vessel's position off Woolpack Buoy at 4.13 p.m. By now the wind was gale- to strong gale-force eight to nine, with rough short seas over the shoals. *Sarah K* was lying bows south with her starboard quarter to the seas.

The lifeboat stood by as a second RAF Sea King helicopter lowered a pump to the casualty. At 4.30 p.m., Coxswain Cox approached the fishing vessel to discuss the position with her skipper, who asked to be towed to King's Lynn but, in the very rough weather, the casualty was too large for the lifeboat to tow. At 5.24 p.m., *Sarah K*'s large foremast broke and, as the helicopters had left the scene, Coxswain Cox decided to take off the crew. A failed attempt was made to go alongside the fishing vessel's port bow but the next approach, made on the starboard side at a steep angle to avoid the trawl doors, was more successful. In the now total darkness, two fishermen were snatched off as the boats rolled together and the lifeboat cleared the casualty by going full astern. Another approach was made when a third man was taken aboard, after which the lifeboat pulled astern and waited for the skipper to check the pumps. At 5.37 p.m. the lifeboat again went alongside and took the skipper off. As soon as he was aboard, Coxswain Cox informed the coastguard that *Sarah K* was adrift, but remained in position as the wind was moderating.

By 6.15 p.m., the wind had dropped to force six so the skipper was put back aboard *Sarah K* and succeeded in anchoring the crippled fishing vessel before being taken back onto the lifeboat which then left the casualty and returned to station. Passage was made via Holkham Bay but, on arrival at Wells at 7.31 p.m., the launching tractor had broken down. The lifeboat was forced to lay off until repairs had been made. For this rescue, the Bronze medal was awarded to Coxswain Cox. Medal service certificates were presented to Second Coxswain Anthony Jordan, Mechanic Albert Court, Assistant Mechanic Alan Cox and crew members Albert Warner, Graham Walker, John Nudds and John Betts.

Towards the end of 1982, the relief lifeboat *Calouste Gulbenkian* was again sent to the station, so *Ernest Tom Neathercoat* could go to Brown's Boatyard at Rowhedge for survey and overhaul. The relief lifeboat was on station from 5 December 1982 to 25 July 1983 during which time she performed five service launches. The most notable of these took place on 11 April 1983, after the 70ft former river tug *Dockman*, which had been on passage from London to Newcastle but whose radar and compass were unserviceable, got into difficulty while being escorted to Wells by the motor fishing vessel *Isabelle Kathleen*. Skipper John Nudds had left Wells in *Isabelle Kathleen* on the morning tide for whelk fishing in the vicinity of Dudgeon Lightvessel. The weather began to deteriorate rapidly, however, and he had just decided to return to harbour when he sighted *Dockman* in difficulties and offered to guide her to Wells.

At 3.25 p.m., when *Isabelle Kathleen* lost contact with *Dockman* in heavy rain squalls, the lifeboat was requested and within fifteen minutes *Calouste Gulbenkian* was launched under the command of Coxswain David Cox. By now the north-easterly wind had risen to strong gale-force nine with very low cloud, constant drizzle and reduced visibility in the rain squalls. The lifeboat made for the harbour mouth and stood by, inside the bar, while *Isabelle Kathleen* entered harbour, the weather having deteriorated to the point where it was unsafe for the fishing vessel to remain at sea. Once *Isabelle Kathleen* was safely in harbour, the lifeboat put to sea. The heavy north-easterly ground swell was producing high steep seas with broken water everywhere, so Coxswain Cox took the lifeboat out of harbour head to sea, only able to make half speed due to the weather. The lifeboat passed directly over the bar and then held a north-westerly course before approaching *Dockman*, which was now in the vicinity of Bridgirdle Buoy.

The tug was sighted at 4.38 p.m. but two minutes later a very large sea hit the lifeboat on the starboard bow, swamped her and filled the cockpit with water up to the necks of those sitting down causing the radar to fail and the VHF radio to work only intermittently. Nevertheless, ten minutes later the lifeboat reached *Dockman*, which was slowly circling around Bridgirdle Buoy waiting for help. With the wind rising to storm-force ten and acting against the tide, in the shallow water around Bridgirdle Buoy the seas were high and steep with the crests constantly breaking. Coxswain Cox immediately advised the tug to follow the lifeboat, with the intention

The lifeboat house as it was in 1986. The extension at the back accommodated the launching tractor, and another addition on the side was used for the inshore lifeboat and crew room. (Nicholas Leach)

In 1983–4, the boathouse was modified to provide a crew room above the ILB house (on right) with access stairs also forming a boarding and viewing platform. The cost of £14,570 was covered by donations from the estate of the late Mrs Annie Newston of Bury St Edmunds and Miss M.H. Mayne of Burnham Market. (Nicholas Leach)

The 37ft Oakley Ernest Tom Neathercoat *launching on exercise in March 1990. (Paul Russell)*

of escorting her to King's Lynn because it was considered too dangerous to try to enter Wells. However, the tug replied that she was short of fuel and her crew were suffering from seasickness so Coxswain Cox altered course to the south-west for Brancaster Roads, where the seas might be easier. The tug also told the lifeboat that she would be unable to put out an anchor so Cox asked that Brancaster fishermen be consulted about entering Brancaster Harbour while the tug continued to follow the lifeboat on a south-westerly course.

Cyril Southerland, skipper of the Brancaster motor fishing vessel *Isabel Deborah*, took his boat out to assess the situation at the entrance to the harbour and informed Wells lifeboat that there was adequate water for the tug to enter harbour and he would act as guide. The lifeboat told the tug to follow her into Brancaster and listen out for *Isabel Deborah* which would guide them both in. At 6.05 p.m., the lifeboat approached the harbour and fifteen minutes later crossed the bar followed by the tug. They then both followed *Isabel Deborah* along the shore towards Brancaster Harbour in heavy beam seas and twenty minutes later were in the harbour under the lee of Scolt Head. As the tug crew were exhausted and the tug's engines, belching black smoke, were failing, the lifeboat went alongside and helped the master anchor his vessel. The lifeboat was placed on a safe mooring for the night, as returning to Wells through the storm was unnecessarily risky. Passage back to Wells was made on 12 April, with the lifeboat reaching station at 6.30 p.m. Repairs were made to the radar and radio, and she was again ready for service on 13 April.

For this excellent service, a framed letter of thanks signed by the Duke of Atholl, chairman of the institution, was presented to Coxswain Cox. Letters of appreciation signed by Rear Admiral W.J. Graham, the RNLI's director, were sent to John Nudds, skipper of the fishing vessel *Isabelle Kathleen*, and Cyril Southerland, skipper of the fishing vessel *Isabel Deborah*.

Somewhat more routine services followed in 1983, 1984 and 1985. On 10 September 1983, *Ernest Tom Neathercoat* was launched to a motor cruiser in difficulties in heavy weather near

Blakeney Overfalls and escorted the vessel into harbour. On 19 January 1984, she went to the aid of the motor fishing vessel *Four Brothers* which had broken down with engine trouble two miles north of Blakeney Harbour in deteriorating weather. By the time the lifeboat reached the casualty, it was under way and so only needed escorting to harbour. On 5 May 1985, the 48ft motor fishing vessel *Thorntree* suffered engine failure near Burnham Flats Buoy so *Ernest Tom Neathercoat* launched at 9.24 p.m. and proceeded at full speed to the casualty. At 11.15 p.m., the lifeboat went alongside the vessel and took off a woman and her twelve-year-old son, then towed the casualty towards Wells. The vessel was anchored off Wells at 3.30 a.m. and brought into harbour at 6.30 a.m. to be berthed.

On 21 November 1986, two motor fishing vessels, *Kenneth William* and *Mor-Nita*, were caught in heavy weather and *Ernest Tom Neathercoat* was requested to stand by. By 7.30 a.m., with conditions very bad, she was launched and proceeded through extremely rough seas to the casualties east of the Fairway Buoy. At 8 a.m., the boats were requested to head west into better water and the lifeboat escorted them, while the coastguard requested helicopter assistance in view of the extreme conditions. Although *Kenneth William* had problems with her engine and her bilge pumps were obstructed by shrimps, these were resolved and she was able to make for Wells Harbour entrance. At 9.38 a.m., the lifeboat and both casualties were making slow progress, with the helicopter escorting them. Once they reached Wells, the sea state was too bad to bring the vessels in so the lifeboat proposed to wait until the weather improved. At 10.27 a.m., the lifeboat, with her drogue rigged, entered harbour to assess conditions and confirmed they were

Although originally open boats offering little protection, apart from a small windscreen, the 37ft Oakleys had additions made to them during their service careers. To improve crew comfort, a folding wheelhouse which enclosed the cockpit was designed and fitted to all Oakleys between 1982 and 1986. It had to fold down as boathouse height was a prime consideration for carriage-launched boats amd no fixed structure could be added above the existing casing top. When this photo of Ernest Tom Neathercoat *being recovered after exercise was taken, the cockpit had been enclosed and radar fitted. (Paul Russell)*

too rough for the casualties. So the lifeboat proceeded back out to sea and lead the casualties to Thornham Bay to shelter. By 12.25 p.m., all three vessels were near Brancaster, in the lee of Gore Middle Sand. At 3.55 p.m., the lifeboat headed east to check the entrance to Brancaster Harbour which, at 5 p.m., the vessels were able to enter with local guidance after which the lifeboat returned to station. She reached Wells at 6 p.m. and waited for the tide before entering harbour and being recovered at 6.45 p.m. after what had been an arduous service.

On 28 November 1986, a week after this service, *Ernest Tom Neathercoat* was taken away from Wells for a major overhaul at Crescent Marine, Otterham Quay, near Rochester. Relief 37ft Oakley *Calouste Gulbenkian* arrived for her third stint at the station and stayed until April 1988 during which time she launched four times on service and saved five lives. The only life-saving service she undertook came on 29 July 1987 when she saved the Dutch yacht *Les Intrigants* and her crew of five. The yacht had gone aground with a fouled propeller to the east of the harbour entrance just after midnight and so at 1.05 a.m. the lifeboat launched. At 1.32 a.m., *Calouste Gulbenkian* was alongside and crew member Allen Frary was transferred to the yacht. The yacht's propeller was freed and the casualty's crew managed to pump out the water which had reached well above the floor boards. The yacht was then slowly towed to the quay and berthed at 7.20 a.m. leaving the lifeboat free to return to the lifeboat house. The other services performed

In August 1986, a new Talus MB-H tractor, T99, arrived at Wells. This sophisticated and powerful vehicle, built in Wales by Bigland, was the latest in a long line of launching tractors used at the station. To accommodate the new vehicle, the tractor house had to be altered and enlarged. (Supplied by Paul Russell)

Relief 37ft Oakley Calouste Gulbenkian *tows in the Dutch yacht* Les Intrigants *and her crew of five after the yacht had gone aground near the harbour entrance on 29 July 1987.*

by *Calouste Gulbenkian* were all more mundane; the last on 1 February 1988, involved assisting the fishing vessel *Viking* of King's Lynn which had broken down in bad weather four miles north of Hunstanton with three persons on board. The lifeboat towed the vessel towards her home port and then transferred the tow the fishing vessel *Portunus* which completed the task of bringing the casualty home.

After sixteen months away, *Ernest Tom Neathercoat* returned to station on 14 April 1988 having had her hull almost completely rebuilt at Crescent Marine with new bulkheads, the engines and machinery overhauled, a new Decca 060 radar and Decca Mk.IV navigator fitted and been completely repainted. The hull replanking was necessary after several of the Oakleys suffered serious hull deterioration problems during the mid-1980s and as a result most were virtually reconstructed. As *Calouste Gulbenkian* had already been replanked, Wells' own boat became low priority which is why she was away for so long. Most Oakleys had been rebuilt in about eight months. But within two months of her return, she was called out to the cabin cruiser *La Mancha* on 27 June 1988. The cruiser had broken down off Blakeney Point and at 3.59 p.m. the lifeboat was launched, heading out through a heavy swell at full speed to find the casualty close inshore off Cley just outside broken water. A tow was successfully passed at 5.25 p.m. and the casualty was pulled offshore and then subsequently towed into Wells Harbour. At 7.40 p.m., as lifeboat and tow passed the lifeboat house, the casualty was able to proceed to the quay under own power.

During 1989, her last full year on station at Wells, *Ernest Tom Neathercoat* undertook several more services to add to her already impressive tally. On 28 March 1989 she went to the local motor fishing vessel *Three Brothers* which was taking in water a mile off Scolt Head. Working with the Hunstanton lifeboat *Spirit of America* (B-556) and a helicopter, she took the vessel in tow and brought her to harbour. Four months later, on 30 July, as weather conditions deteriorated, *Ernest Tom Neathercoat* had a busy afternoon assisting Sheringham and Cromer lifeboats off Blakeney after sailing vessels and a safety boat were caught out in bad weather. Various yachts

Ernest Tom Neathercoat *on display in the car park at the end of Beach Road in 1998. (Nicholas Leach)*

and fishing vessels were in difficulty including *Sea Quest, Ma Freen, Sharon* and *Fair Chance* from Wells which *Ernest Tom Neathercoat* stood by as they entered harbour. She then proceeded to sea again to escort the remaining casualties, with Cromer lifeboat towing the yachts *Serena* and *Marlet,* and Sheringham lifeboat *Manchester Unity of Oddfellows* (ON.960) towing *Meg.* She escorted the lifeboats and their casualties into Wells, then returned to sea to escort any further vessels in difficulty before returning to be recovered at 7.20 p.m. Cromer lifeboat remained at Wells until the weather had improved.

The last effective service performed by *Ernest Tom Neathercoat* at Wells took place on 14 September 1989. At 4.26 p.m., Yarmouth Coastguard advised the station that a yacht, *Amber Crest,* was aground on Wells bar and they were concerned for safety. Just over ten minutes later, both lifeboat and inshore lifeboat were launched. The inshore lifeboat *Jane Ann,* escorted into harbour by the lifeboat, towed the casualty to a mooring and the lifeboat returned to station at 5.23 p.m. She did put out again on 2 May 1990 to a stranded yacht, but her services were not needed, and two months later she was replaced at the station by a new lifeboat.

When the Oakleys were taken out of service, they were deemed unsuitable for private sale because of the unusual self-righting system and the RNLI adopted a policy whereby the sale would only be agreed if the boat was going on static display and not used afloat. Where a suitable buyer could not be found, the boats were broken up. When *Ernest Tom Neathercoat* left Wells, she was sent to North Sunderland for a short spell, from August 1990 to 1991, before being taken to the National Boat Building Centre at Oulton Broad, near Lowestoft, in 1992 and displayed in the car park there for six years. She was then moved back to Wells and placed on display in the car park at the end of Beach Road, close to the lifeboat house in which she had spent so many years. In September 2000, she was moved to a farm not far from the town and remains there awaiting restoration and further display.

six

Doris M. Mann of Ampthill

12-003

On 3 July 1990, the new 12m Mersey *Doris M. Mann of Ampthill* (ON.1161) was declared operational at Wells. The Mersey class had been designed and developed by the RNLI during the 1980s for stations where the lifeboat is carriage-launched, in order to replace the 37ft Oakley and 37ft 6in Rother lifeboats which were at the end of their operational lives. The new design represented a major technological advance over the Oakley class and, powered by twin 285hp Caterpillar 3208T turbo-charged diesels, was capable of speeds in excess of seventeen knots, about twice that of the Oakley. Approximately 245 gallons of fuel were carried giving a range, at full speed, of 145 nautical miles. The design was self-righting by virtue of the inherent buoyancy of the watertight wheelhouse, which also contained permanent seating for the crew of six, with an additional seat for a doctor and the latest navigation and communication equipment was fitted. The first eight boats of the class, including that for Wells, were constructed from aluminium, but later boats were made from fibre reinforced composite (FRC).

To enable the boat to be launched from a beach, the propellers were protected by the hull form which incorporated a tunnel stern and extended bilge keels that supported the weight of the boat on the beach, preventing propellers and rudders from damage. Following the introduction of the Mersey into the RNLI's fleet, a target date of 1993 was set by when it was intended to have lifeboats capable of at least fifteen knots operating from every station equipped with an all-weather lifeboat and this, of course, included Wells. The station received

The new Wells lifeboat Doris M. Mann of Ampthill *under construction at FBM Ltd, Cowes, 1989. (Paul Russell)*

The new Wells lifeboat Doris
M. Mann of Ampthill
*undergoing her self-righting
trials at Cowes, February
1990. For the trial, the boat
was hauled over by a crane
and the strops were then
released with the boat righting
herself in about six seconds.
The righting capability came
from the inherent buoyancy
of the wheelhouse. The trial
was filmed and shown on
BBC's* Blue Peter *television
programme, and was
introduced by presenter Diane
Louise Jordan.
(Paul Russell)*

Shortly after she had been completed, the new Wells lifeboat Doris M. Mann of Ampthill *was displayed at the London Boat Show in 1990 as the centrepiece of the RNLI's stand. A brass plaque on timber backing inside the lifeboat reads 'This Lifeboat was provided from the bequest of Miss Doris May Mann of Ampthill 1990'. (Nicholas Leach)*

Doris M. Mann of Ampthill *arrives at Wells for the first time in June 1990. After a period of crew training at the station, she was declared operational on 3 July 1990. (EDP, supplied by Paul Russell)*

the first production Mersey, numbered 12-003, after the two earlier boats had been designated pre-production prototypes although both subsequently entered service. Construction began in late 1988 at FBM Ltd in Cowes, Isle of Wight, and she was completed in November 1989. A series of trials, including a self righting programme in February 1990, followed with the main trials programme held during March 1990, while dockside, speed and fuel trials taking place the following month. Following a final paint, the last trials programme began on 17 May 1990 after which she was sailed to the RNLI depot at Poole.

Before the lifeboat was sent to Wells, Coxswain/Mechanic Graham Walker, Second Coxswain Allen Frary, Assistant Mechanic Sonnie Warner, Emergency Mechanic Michael Frary and crew members James Case and David Pentney-Smith took part in a sea training course at RNLI Headquarters, Poole, from 18 to 22 June 1990. To learn about the new boat's capabilities, the Wells lifeboatmen carried out various practical exercises while also studying the lifeboat's construction and design in the training centre in Poole. Practical exercises covered the use communications, radar and navigation equipment. Emergency procedures, such as man overboard drill, fire fighting, engine and steering failure were practised, as well as a winching drill with a search and rescue helicopter. Once the course had been completed, the crew sailed to Wells with Tom Nutman, divisional inspector of lifeboats for the east, in command.

The new lifeboat had been funded from a legacy of more than £1 million left by the late Doris Mann specifically for a new lifeboat for the town. A former Alderman and JP, Doris Mann had a row of quayside cottages in Wells where she had spent her holidays for thirty years watching the fishing boats at the quay. Miss Mann, of Ampthill, who died aged eighty-four, asked for the boat to be named after herself. She had been a life-long supporter of the RNLI, helping her parents to raise funds for the service for the first time in the 1920s. At the time of her death in December 1988, she was president of the RNLI Ampthill Branch, ran an RNLI shop from one of her properties in the town and in 1985 was awarded an Honorary Life Governorship, the RNLI's highest honour for volunteer fundraisers.

The new lifeboat was formally named during a ceremony at the quay on 17 July 1990. Derek Styman, chairman of the Wells Branch, opened proceedings with Anthony Northey speaking on behalf of the donor and formally handing over the lifeboat to Michael Vernon, chairman of the RNLI. In turn, Mr Vernon passed her into the care of Honorary Secretary David Case, after which a vote of thanks was proposed by Margaret Gerken, Chairman of the Wells Ladies' Lifeboat Guild. The service of dedication was led by the Revd William Sayer, Rector of St Nicholas Parish Church and lifeboat chaplain, assisted by the Revd John Weaver, the Revd Colin Riches and Pastor Bill Barton. At the close of the service, Her Royal Highness the Duchess of Kent named the lifeboat Doris M. Mann of Ampthill and the boat was then taken to sea for a short demonstration run.

To accommodate the new lifeboat, the boathouse had to be altered considerably. The house had already been altered and modified several times for successive new lifeboats, including in 1965 for the then new 37ft Oakley, but the changes in 1990 to accommodate the new 12m Mersey were considerably more extensive. The house was virtually rebuilt with greatly improved accommodation for boat, tractor, inshore lifeboat and crew. Further improvements were implemented in the mid-1990s when work on the timber revetment and groynes was undertaken to prevent erosion of the sandy headland on which the boathouse is sited. Greenheart timber from Guyana was used having been taken from the recently demolished slipway at Eastbourne. In 1998, further new groynes were installed to retain the beach protecting the boathouse.

After three launches that did not result in rescues – on 14 July 1990 to Flying Dutchman, on 15 August to flares and on 17 August to an aircraft – the first effective service by Doris M. Mann of Ampthill came on 23 August 1990. She went to the fishing vessel Sheena Mackay which was

Doris M. Mann of Ampthill at Wells Quay during her naming ceremony on 17 July 1990. She was named by HRH the Duchess of Kent and is pictured with the duchess and other invited guests aboard. (Jeff Morris)

The scene at Wells Quay during the naming ceremony of Doris M. Mann of Ampthill on 17 July 1990, with Sheringham lifeboat Manchester Unity of Oddfellows (ON.960) also in attendance. (Jeff Morris)

Doris M. Mann of Ampthill on service to the yacht Leveret *on 15 June 1991. She launched to the yacht at 8.05 p.m. and found the casualty about a mile off Stiffkey. The lifeboat went alongside twice to take off crew and put two lifeboatmen aboard ready for a tow which ended with the boat being brought into Wells Harbour just after 10 p.m. This was only the third effective service undertaken by the 12m Mersey.*

taking in water near the North Race Buoy and found the casualty two hours after launching off Titchwell with an RAF helicopter in attendance. The vessel was taken in tow and by 9.30 p.m. Wells Harbour had been reached. The casualty was escorted to the quay and soon after 10 p.m. the lifeboat had been recovered.

On 16 October 1991, *Doris M. Mann of Ampthill* was involved in a much longer service. She launched to the motor fishing vessel *Cerealia* which was taking in water six and a half miles north of Wells in rough seas and force eight to nine winds. An RAF helicopter had put a pump on board the casualty but a lifeboat escort was requested so at 10.09 a.m. the lifeboat launched, reaching the casualty near Bridgirdle Buoy eight minutes later, and stood by waiting for high water so the casualty could be escorted to Wells Harbour. At 12.50 p.m. one of the lifeboat's crew, James Case, was transferred to the casualty for the attempt to get into the harbour. But when the casualty touched bottom inside No.1 Buoy, it was realised that getting into Wells would be too difficult and dangerous in view of the neap tides and strong wind, which was forecast to increase to severe gale force.

Before proceeding to sea with *Cerealia*, the lifeboat assisted the local fishing vessel *Mor-Nita* which had gone aground. After towing it off, it reached the harbour unaided. The lifeboat crew then turned their attention to *Cerealia*. Once clear of the harbour, the casualty's two crew were taken off, both wet and cold, and lifeboatman Jimmy Wright was transferred to the casualty. At about 2.30 p.m. the lifeboat's own salvage pump was put on board, along with a third crew

Graham Walker, coxswain from 1989 to 1997, on right with Second Coxswain Allen Frary during recovery at Holkham Beach, Christmas Eve 1993. Graham joined the crew in 1962, became mechanic in 1982, second coxswain/mechanic in 1987 and coxswain/ mechanic two years later. He was awarded the MBE in the 1997 New Year's Honours and before becoming full time in 1982, had various jobs and was at one time Wells harbour master. (Campbell MacCallum)

member, Fred Whitaker, as the casualty was still taking on water in very rough conditions about two miles east of the Woolpack Buoy. Two hours later, the casualty experienced engine problems and so was taken in tow again, for a further two hours, before being anchored at King's Lynn No.5 Buoy. There the two boats waited for the flood tide before proceeding to King's Lynn. At 10.15 p.m. the two craft reached their destination and the casualty was berthed at Purfleet Quay, after which the lifeboat refuelled and proceeded down river heading back to station. She entered Wells Harbour at 2.05 a.m. and ten minutes later was being recovered after a testing service for which Letters of Thanks were sent by the RNLI chairman to Coxswain/Mechanic Graham Walker and crewman James Case. Director's Letters of Thanks were sent to Second Coxswain Allen Frary, Assistant Mechanic Michael Frary, and Fred Whitaker, James Wright and Darren Hume. The letters were formally presented on 2 February 1991 by actor Roy Marsden.

Doris M. Mann of Ampthill undertook a number of routine services during 1992 and in 1993 was away from the station during the early summer for a routine refit at Crescent Marine, Gillingham. In her place came relief 12m Mersey *Marine Engineer* (ON.1169) which was involved in a night time service on 5 July 1993. She launched at 10.33 p.m. to the yacht *Rocking Horse*, which was in difficulty. With the weather forecast to deteriorate the following day, the lifeboat took the yacht in tow but, because of the low tide, had to wait until the following morning to bring her down to the quay. She was brought alongside just before 7.20 a.m. on 6 July and the lifeboat returned to station an hour later.

To accommodate the new 12m Mersey lifeboat, the boathouse was completely rebuilt and enlarged in 1989–90. On the west side, the house was expanded and a workshop for the mechanic was put in with a drying room above. The roof of the main boathouse was removed and replaced by a much higher steel structure. The main boathouse was extended to the north and new doors were fitted, and the old crew room was converted into a souvenir outlet. (Paul Russell)

The lifeboat house built originally in the 1890s after being completely rebuilt almost a century later for the new 12m Mersey lifeboat. Following the completion of the structural and internal rebuilding, the outside was stripped and reclad with plastic coated moulded aluminium leaving it bearing little resemblance to the original house. (Nicholas Leach)

Doris M. Mann of Ampthill returned from refit on 25 July and, during the last leg of her passage from Lowestoft, was asked to assist the yacht *Starlight Spehull* which had a broken rudder in the Hewett Gas Field in very rough seas and force seven to nine winds. She reached the casualty at 11.15 a.m. and found it was being towed by the Lowestoft fishing vessel *Leander*. Ten minutes later, the lifeboat took over the tow and set course for Wells. At one point the tow line broke so had to be reconnected, while the lifeboat crew became increasingly concerned for the welfare of the owner, an elderly gentleman, partially paralysed, who was suffering from hypothermia. The rescue helicopter was requested to help and, with great difficulty, airlifted the casualty off his vessel using the hi-line technique. As the owner was being winched clear of the boat, the tow rope parted again so Second Coxswain Allen Frary was put aboard to re-establish the tow. At 1.25 p.m., with the tow secured again, both vessels proceeded to Wells in heavy thundery squalls. At 7 p.m., they had reached the Wells Fairway Buoy and waited for the tide. At 10 p.m., the relief lifeboat *Marine Engineer* launched and escorted both vessels into harbour, with the casualty eventually getting to the quays just before 11 p.m. The lifeboat returned to her station at midnight after a long passage and the relief boat left the station on 26 July for duty at Skegness. For the service to the yacht *Starlight Spehull*, Letters of Thanks signed by the RNLI chairman were presented to Coxswain/Mechanic Graham Walker and Second Coxswain Allen Frary.

Less than two weeks after this service, on 5 August 1993 another rescue was undertaken in heavy weather. From about 1 p.m., Coxswain/Mechanic Graham Walker had been monitoring

Lifeboat crew posing with lifeboat and inshore lifeboat for the RNLI's 1994 legacy calendar. (By courtesy of RNLI)

Above: Doris M. Mann of Ampthill *approaches the mock 'casualty', Pescarus, during a medical exercise in September 1994 with the crew making the boat ready to come alongside. (Nicholas Leach)*

Left: *Second Coxswain Allen Frary (wearing RNLI life-jacket) attends to the injured people during a medical exercise with* Doris M. Mann of Ampthill *escorting the vessel* Pescarus, *which was acting as the casualty, down the channel and into harbour. (Nicholas Leach)*

D class inflatable D-352 Jane Ann *which was sent to Wells in 1988 and served until November 1996. A 16ft 3in Avon EA16 type inshore lifeboat, she was funded by an anonymous benefactor. (Nicholas Leach)*

the yacht *Pussy Galore* which was ashore on a sand bar about half a mile east of Wells Harbour with a failed outboard. A few hours later, as the yacht was still in difficulty, both all-weather and inshore lifeboats were launched. D-352 *Jane Ann* set off at 6.56 p.m. and put a crew man on board to secure a tow. *Doris M. Mann of Ampthill* launched ten minutes later with the wind gale-force eight gusting to force nine and took the casualty in tow, with the ILB following astern. At 7.20 p.m., the ILB was hit by an unusually big sea and forced vertically up on her stern before falling sideways and throwing two crewmen, Fred Whitaker and Gary Wright, into the water. crewman Richard Warner managed to stay in contact with the boat and soon assisted the other two back aboard. The engine was restarted, the crew were checked by those on the all-weather boat, and the ILB then resumed station astern of casualty. Five minutes later the boats entered harbour, the tow was passed to the ILB and the casualty was secured at 7.44 p.m.

During the mid-1990s, the station continued the work of life-saving without being called on to perform any particularly dramatic rescues. In the early hours of 25 July 1994, *Doris M. Mann of Ampthill* launched to the rigid-inflatable *Cambridge Divers* which had been caught out by a violent thunderstorm off Blakeney and so was brought to safety. In the early hours of 13 August 1995, the lifeboat launched to the fishing vessel *Katherine Lucy* which was taking on water and losing power in the South Race Buoy area. The vessel was taken in tow to King's Lynn as her draft was too deep for Wells Harbour. At 6.37 p.m. on 4 August 1996, the lifeboat launched to the motor cruiser *Starry Vere* at East Docking Buoy after her skipper had requested assistance because the crew were sick and frightened. *Doris M. Mann of Ampthill* escorted the boat to sheltered water where Second Coxswain Allen Frary went aboard to pilot the casualty up to the quay.

On 17 November 1996, *Doris M. Mann of Ampthill* was launched into force seven to eight winds and rough seas after red flares near Wells Harbour bar had been sighted by workers on board the dredger *Wallbrook*. The motor fishing vessel *Remus* with three crew was in difficulty having lost power in heavy breaking seas. At 8.20 p.m., five minutes after launching, the coxswain

The new D class inflatable D-512 Jane Ann II is launched at the end of her naming ceremony on 15 June 1997 with Doris M. Mann of Ampthill forming the backdrop. She replaced D-352 in November 1996 and was funded from the gift of Mrs Jan Branford, Sudbury, Suffolk, who named the boat herself. (Nicholas Leach)

The new inshore lifeboat D-512 Jane Ann II is put through her paces for a short demonstration after her naming ceremony on 15 June 1997 for the benefit of the supporters. (Paul Russell)

Relief 12m Mersey Peggy and Alex Caird *(ON.1124) launching from the beach in August 1998. She was on station from July to October 1998 while the station boat went for refit. During her time at Wells, the relief lifeboat undertook three effective services, two in August 1998 and the last on 11 October when she escorted the fishing vessel* Buzzard *towards King's Lynn after it had developed engine trouble off Brancaster.* Peggy and Alex Caird *was also on station during the rally of former lifeboats held at Wells on 2 August 1998. (Nicholas Leach)*

Peggy and Alex Caird *heading towards the quay to attend a fund-raising event. Built in 1988, she was the first Mersey type lifeboat and served at Bridlington for seven years before being placed in the Relief Fleet. (Nicholas Leach)*

requested helicopter assistance and at 8.35 p.m. the tractor was taken along the shore to a position close to the casualty taking shore helpers and crewmen Jason Walker and Tim Rumbles in dry suits. A rocket line was fired from the lifeboat to the shore and the crew in dry suits were able to use this to reach the casualty, assist one crewman ashore and attach the tow line, leaving the vessel's skipper and the other crew member on board. At 9.15 p.m. the helicopter arrived as the lifeboat began the tow to deeper water so illuminated the casualty and stood by until deep water had been reached. The tow was then continued to Wells Harbour and at 10.15 p.m. the casualty was made fast at the quay after which the lifeboat returned to station. For this excellent service, a letter of thanks was sent by the RNLI to the station in recognition of the crew's efforts.

Every year, an annual lifeboat service is held at Wells Quay when the lifeboat is brought down from the boathouse for a religious service which is accompanied by the local brass band. On 17 August 1997, *Doris M. Mann of Ampthill* had attended the service as usual, but just as it was ending she was asked to assist the catamaran *Alleycat* which was unsure of its position due to a compass failure. The lifeboat headed to sea complete with crew, retired crew, medical auxiliaries, and three vicars to find the casualty about two miles west of Wells Harbour. The second coxswain was put on board to pilot the catamaran into the harbour, ending an eventful day and the first Annual Lifeboat Service for Allen Frary as coxswain/mechanic, who had been appointed to the full-time post on 27 July 1997. Previously a whelk fisherman in the family business, skippering two boats *Amethyst* and *Alison Christine*, he joined the crew on 16 September 1976 and became second coxswain on 22 February 1989 before becoming coxswain.

Doris M. Mann of Ampthill returned from a refit at West Custom Marine, Lymington, on 22 October 1998, having come from the south coast via Newhaven, Ramsgate and Lowestoft. The following day, relief lifeboat *Peggy and Alex Caird* (ON.1124), which was at Wells from July to September 1998, sailed to Grimsby for repairs at Leggett's Yard. Within ten days of her return,

On 15 August 1999, a number of ex-lifeboats gathered as part of the town's annual Harbour Day, following a similar get-together the previous year. All under private ownership, the former lifeboats pictured are, left to right, Mary Gabriel *(ex-ON.1000),* Arklow *(ex-ON.807* Inbhear Mor*),* Constance of Blakeney *(ex-ON.967* Dorothy and Philip Constant*) and* Sareter *(ex-ON.770* Harriot Dixon*). (Paul Russell)*

Inshore lifeboat D-512 Jane Ann II *pulls in the motor boat* Marsh Martin *which had capsized on the bar in August 1998. The ILB saved the crew of two and a dog, brought them ashore, and then returned to bring in the empty boat, a routine service but typical of the kind of work for which the ILB is ideally suited. (Paul Russell)*

Doris M. Mann of Ampthill *at West Custom Marine, Lymington, undergoing refit in 1998. (Peter Edey)*

Allen Frary, coxswain since 1997, having served as second coxswain for eight years. Wells born and bred, Allen left school and joined the merchant navy in 1968. After a couple of years working ashore, he went back to sea and began whelk fishing in 1976, the same year that he first joined the lifeboat crew.

Doris M. Mann of Ampthill was called into action. She launched on 31 October 1998 to the motor boat *Marynett*, which was in difficulty west of Blakeney Harbour while on passage to Wells from Yarmouth. The casualty was towed to Wells and entered the harbour on the first of the flood tide. The skipper then assured Coxswain Allen Frary that his outboard motor was powerful enough to gain steerage whilst crossing the bar but the ILB was launched to stand by. As the motor boat entered the channel, heavy swell picked it up and a large wave drove it ashore. The launching tractor was used to connect a tow to the boat and refloat it, after which it continued to the quay under its own power. The lifeboat was rehoused at 12.15 a.m. after a service lasting almost six hours.

The following year, 1999, proved to be very busy, with three services undertaken in April. On 3 April, *Doris M. Mann of Ampthill* towed in the yacht *Stella Maris* and her crew of two after the casualty had requested assistance following a power failure leaving the radio not working and the vessel drifting in fog in the Wash area. On 9 April, the motor fishing vessel *Shangri-La* was towed in after it had lost all power and was taking on water. And on 11 April, the fishing vessel *La Belle Helene* broke down off Wells Harbour with a split fuel tank. But as the vessel was 40ft in length with a draft of 6ft, neap tides prevented her from getting into the harbour. So Coxswain Allen Frary requested help from the Humber lifeboat *Pride of the Humber* (ON.1216) to take the casualty into Grimsby. With the Humber lifeboat on her way, a tow was established and Wells lifeboat towed the vessel at about four knots, having to contend with winds gusting to thirty-two knots accompanied by heavy swells. Wells lifeboat rendezvoused with the Humber lifeboat at Scott Patch Buoy where the tow was transferred, and the Wells boat returned to station.

Doris M. Mann of Ampthill and Ernest Tom Neathercoat with crew members past and present on Sunday 21 May 2000 to mark the Millennium. The past and present crew, shorehelpers and committee members had a combined service to the Wells station and RNLI amounting to more than 1,000 years. (Campbell MacCallum)

The all-weather lifeboat's only effective service of 2000 took place on 2 September after Coxswain Allen Frary became concerned for the 17ft yacht *Candy*, which was attempting to enter the harbour through shallow rough water. D class inflatable *Jane Ann II* had been launched to assist with Bob Smith at the helm and managed to escort the yacht through rough and confused seas to calmer water. Meanwhile, *Doris M. Mann of Ampthill* had launched at 7.35 p.m. and two children were transferred to her from the yacht. Two lifeboatmen were then put on board the casualty to work with the skipper, who remained on board, to secure a tow. The lifeboat towed the casualty for two miles, much of the time with the sea on her beam resulting in considerable pitching and rolling in the force five to six winds and rough seas with water coming on board and making the casualty difficult to control.

As the tow approached Wells, the ILB was sent to the harbour entrance to stand by in slightly calmer conditions and it was dark by the time the lifeboat and casualty approached the outer harbour. Just as the lifeboat brought the casualty to the entrance, a big sea swept over it carrying the skipper overboard. Fortunately the lifeboat's searchlight kept him in sight and the ILB was quickly alerted to pick him up. He was then brought to the lifeboat house where, together with the two children, he was treated for shock and hypothermia. The yacht, which was almost sinking by the time it reached the harbour, was towed in by the lifeboat and beached. For their

For the service to the yacht Candy on 2 September 2000, Bob Smith and Allen Frary were accorded the Thanks of the Institution Inscribed on Vellum and the crew received Vellum Service Certificates. Tractor driver Phil Eaglen was presented with the Chairman's Letter of Thanks. Pictured left to right are: Alfie Smith, Allen Frary, Jason Walker, Mark White, Phil Eaglen and Alan Platten. (By courtesy of Wells Lifeboat Station)

D class inflatable D-512 Jane Ann II, on station since 1996, with Mark Frary (helm), Tracy Fletcher, Stuart Garner and Regan Smith on board during a routine exercise. (Nicholas Leach)

efforts during this service, the Thanks on Vellum was accorded to Coxswain Frary and Second Coxswain Smith, and Vellum Service Certificates were presented to the rest of the crew; Assistant Mechanic Michael Frary, Alfred Smith, Nicky King, James Walker, Mark White, Alan Platten, Kevin Parr, Gary Wright and Martin Emerson. Tractor driver Phil Eaglen, who was the first to spot *Candy* in trouble, received a letter of appreciation from the RNLI's operations director.

After a series of routine services in 2001, on 8 September that year *Doris M. Mann of Ampthill* and her crew were involved in a testing rescue after the yacht *Costley* was reported disabled with a broken rudder two miles north of Wells in rough seas and force eight winds. The lifeboat reached the casualty at 11.11 p.m. and transferred crew member Nicky King across with a casualty drogue. RAF Rescue helicopter R128 provided stand-by cover while the crewman secured a tow and deployed the drogue. The tow commenced at 11.30 p.m. and an hour and a half later both lifeboat and casualty entered the Wells buoyed channel. The yacht was then taken down to the quay and secured there, with the lifeboat returning to station early the following morning.

The first two services of 2002 proved to be lengthy rescues. On 9 January 2002, the ILB launched to the fishing vessel *Zuiderzee* which was taking in more water than her pumps could cope with in only slight seas. At 10.53 a.m. *Doris M. Mann of Ampthill* was launched and Sheringham lifeboat *Manchester Unity of Oddfellows* (B-702) was also called. A few minutes later, Sheringham lifeboat was alongside the casualty with Wells lifeboat quickly on scene as well. By this time, the water was rising more quickly and the situation was rapidly deteriorating so Wells lifeboat's pump was transferred onto the casualty which stemmed the ingress of water. With a tow prepared, Sheringham lifeboat was released from the scene. Because the casualty was too large to berth at Wells, the lifeboat headed east. By 1.30 p.m., the tow was proceeding at about

Doris M. Mann of Ampthill *and the fishing vessel* Charles William *attempt unsuccessfully to get the trip vessel* Albatros *afloat on 2 May 2002. The vessel ran aground on 27 April 2002, the day after the lifeboat had assisted her in heavy weather, and remained stuck for two months. (Campbell MacCallum)*

*Lifeboat crew and station officials on 25 March 2003 pictured to mark the retirement of crew member
Alfie Smith. A copy of the photo was presented to him in the crewroom after the practice launch that day.
Pictured from front to back, left to right, are: Coxswain/Mechanic Allen Frary, Deputy Second Coxswain
Nicky King, Second Mechanic Michael Frary, Alfie Smith, Mark Frary, Matthew Owen, Mark Trett, Alan
Platten, Honorary Secretary Richard Cracknell, DLA Peter Rainsford, DLA Chris Hardy, Richard Platten,
Andrew Spiers, Max Phillips, Regan Smith, Deputy Second Coxswain Greg Hewitt, Assistant Tractor
Driver Desmond Wright, Paula Andrews, Darren Eaglen, Shaun Edwards, Malcolm Smith, Kent Cooper,
Tractor Driver Phil Eaglen, Phil Raisbury, Robin Golding, Darren Thompson, Head Launcher Paul Wick,
Kevin Parr, and Deputy Head Launcher Nicky Beck. (Campbell MacCallum)*

Changeover at Wells on 25 August 2003 with relief lifeboat Royal Shipwright *(ON.1162), on left, changing places with* Doris M. Mann of Ampthill *which went to Lymington for a full refit, including the installation of a new fire extinguisher system. She left Wells on 29 August and was taken via Harwich, Ramsgate and Newhaven arriving at Green Marine on 1 September 2003. (Peter Edey)*

Recovery of relief lifeboat Royal Shipwright *in August 2003 after she had arrived at the station to take the place of* Doris M. Mann of Ampthill *for a couple of months. (Peter Edey)*

Relief 12m Mersey Royal Shipwright *(ON. 1162) emerges from the boathouse ready for an exercise launch on 28 September 2003. The relief Mersey was more or less identical to Wells' own lifeboat. (Nicholas Leach)*

Relief 12m Mersey Royal Shipwright *(ON. 1162) on exercise off Wells Harbour. (Nicholas Leach)*

On board Doris M. Mann of Ampthill *in May 2003 are the crew who took part in the* Albatros *service on 26 April 2002. Coxswain Allen Frary was awarded the Chairman's Letter of Thanks for the rescue, and the crew received the Chief Executive's Letter of Thanks. Pictured from left to right are: Nicky King, Michael Frary, Mark Frary, Bob Smith, Allen Frary and Alfie Smith. Also on that service but not pictured were Gary Wright and Greg Hewitt.*

seven knots and the Lowestoft lifeboat *Spirit of Lowestoft* (ON.1132) had been requested to take over the tow. The transfer to the Lowestoft lifeboat took place at 2.45 p.m. while Cromer lifeboat *Ruby and Arthur Reed II* (ON.1097) was also launched to provide an additional pump for the casualty. At 3.10 p.m., *Doris M. Mann of Ampthill* was released and was recovered at 5 p.m. after a service that had taken all day.

On 26 April 2002, the Dutch registered motor vessel *Albatros*, which operates as a charter vessel out of Wells, left the port with a crew of four and seven passengers for a day sail. As she anchored off awaiting the tide after returning in the afternoon, the weather deteriorated with squalls of force six to seven and she started to drag her anchor. When she tried to weigh anchor, her starboard anchor became fouled and she did not have sufficient power to make headway into the strong headwind and swell. The fishing boat *Pathfinder* established a tow but making headway was no easier and during the tow, *Albatros* was pushed onto the east side of the channel in broken water. The skipper of *Pathfinder* was forced to abandon the tow and lifeboat assistance was requested.

At 6.31 p.m., *Doris M. Mann of Ampthill* launched and ten minutes later attempted to pass a tow, having to go alongside twice to pass a heaving line. Bringing the lifeboat round to weather and negotiating the anchor chain, Coxswain Allen Frary stationed the lifeboat ahead of the casualty and took up the strain on the tow. But the wind, tide and sea swung the lifeboat along the starboard side of *Albatros* and Coxswain Frary had to cut the tow to get the lifeboat clear. So a new tow was passed and although the lifeboat was again swung round by wind and tide, this time the crew of *Albatros* slipped the tow so it could be retrieved before the lifeboat got clear. The third attempt to get a tow aboard proved rather difficult after the heaving line wound round the casualty's anchor chain. During a sudden squall which then pushed *Albatros* over, the anchor chain almost damaged the skeg of the lifeboat but when the chain slacked the lifeboat was slowly driven ahead and safely cleared it.

Although another tow was rigged, the casualty was still finding it impossible to lift its port anchor and breaking seas threatened to force the lifeboat to starboard and down the side of *Albatros*. The anchor chain could not be slipped or cut due to an equipment failure until, after forty-five minutes, the chain was finally retrieved and the tow began. The lifeboat was able to bring the vessel into the broken water on the west side of the channel. At times, the lifeboat and casualty had to contend with breaking seas as they crossed the bar and the life-jacket of one lifeboatman inflated under the pressure of water breaking over the deck of the lifeboat. Although the chart table was broken when a sea crashed through *Albatros'* wheelhouse door, the rest of the tow was uneventful and the charter vessel was anchored in sheltered water after which the lifeboat took off the seven passengers and brought them ashore at the boathouse before being rehoused at 8.50 p.m.

Doris M. Mann of Ampthill undertook several more services during 2002, although none were as testing as the *Albatros* rescue. On 4 June, she brought in the yacht *Amurus* and four days later assisted the charter fishing vessel *Desert Moon* which had suffered engine failure twenty miles offshore. The next day, she launched to the barge *De-Hoop 3* which was on a delivery voyage from Lowestoft to King's Lynn and was unable to make headway against the tide and wind off Burnham Flats. The lifeboat escorted the barge into sheltered waters ending a busy few days for her crew. Another call came on 1 July to escort the yacht *Sing High* with the final service of the year taking place on 31 August to the motor vessel *Jennifer*, which was on passage from Lowestoft to Hull with two persons on board when her engine broke down in bad weather. The vessel's windshield was smashed by strong waves and she started taking on water. Two lifeboatmen, Second Coxswain Bob Smith and Deputy Second Coxswain Nicky King, were transferred to the vessel, along with a pump, and at 10.45 a.m. a tow was commenced back to Wells. The casualty was moored at the quay at 1.15 p.m. and the lifeboat returned to station.

Presentation to Honorary Secretary Richard Cracknell on 28 February 2004 on the occasion of his retirement. Pictured are, left to right: Coxswain Allen Frary, Richard Cracknell, Divisional Inspector Martyn Smith and Peter Rainsford, who became honorary secretary (now termed lifeboat operations manager) in Richard's place. (Cambell MacCallum)

Doris M. Mann of Ampthill brings in the small yacht Cygnus *on 23 May 2004 with relief D class inflatable D-446 standing by. The yacht got into difficulty in short, steep seas at the entrance to the harbour and the lifeboat, which was on exercise at the time, towed her into calmer waters before resuming her exercise. (Nicholas Leach)*

Relief D class inflatable D-446 Holme Team, with Shaun Edwards (helm), Max Phillips, Phil Raisbury and Darren Eaglen on board, clears the breakers at the bar while on exercise, May 2004. (Nicholas Leach)

Doris M. Mann of Ampthill *crosses the bar on exercise, May 2004. (Nicholas Leach)*

On 24 May 2003, *Doris M. Mann of Ampthill* undertook a routine service to the fishing vessel *Ma Freen*, which had engine failure. A low water launch at 7.57 a.m. was undertaken and the lifeboat reached the casualty at 9.50 a.m. Five minutes later a tow was commenced towards Wells in smooth conditions at eight knots, with lifeboat and casualty arriving at Wells Fairway Buoy at 1.10 p.m. Meanwhile, Cromer lifeboat *Ruby and Arthur Reed II* had launched to assist another vessel, the yacht *Rambling Rose*, which was on passage from Lowestoft to Grimsby when it suffered engine failure north of Trimingham. Cromer lifeboat towed the yacht towards Wells and, once the Wells lifeboat had completed the *Ma Freen* service, the lifeboats met off Cley-next-the-Sea to transfer the tow to *Doris M. Mann of Ampthill*. The transfer took place at 2.13 p.m. and the casualty was safely moored at Wells Quay an hour and a half later.

On 25 August 2003, relief lifeboat *Royal Shipwright* (ON.1162) arrived at Wells so that *Doris M. Mann of Ampthill* could go to Green Marine at Lymington for overhaul. The relief lifeboat undertook four services during her time at the station, launching three times in September. Her first call came on 1 September when she went to a sailing dinghy with two persons on board that had been capsized in strong northerly winds and heavy swell on the bar at Blakeney and was being swept out to sea. The casualty was quickly located, having drifted outside the harbour entrance, and the two persons were safely taken on board the lifeboat. Sheringham ILB was also on hand and recovered the dinghy while its occupants were landed at Wells. On 22 September, *Royal Shipwright* was again called out after a sudden storm developed off the Norfolk coast. She launched at 3.27 p.m. to the yacht *Tequila*, which had requested urgent assistance after engine failure, and reached the casualty at Brancaster at 4.15 p.m. by which time it had grounded on the lee shore. After two attempts to get it off, the lifeboat successfully towed it into deeper water in the approaches to Brancaster Harbour and then to the safety of Brancaster Staithe at 5.34 p.m.

Doris M. Mann of Ampthill *being launched on exercise from the boathouse into the channel at the harbour mouth using the Talus MB-H tractor T99. (Nicholas Leach)*

The retaining chains are slipped and Doris M. Mann of Ampthill *slides off the carriage at the end of the launching procedure. (Nicholas Leach)*

Doris M. Mann of Ampthill *leaving the lifeboat station on exercise. She usually launches on exercise once every two weeks. (Nicholas Leach)*

Doris M. Mann of Ampthill returned from refit on 24 January 2004 having left Lymington on 21 January, and *Royal Shipwright* departed for another relief duty. The year proved to be a quiet one with four effective services completed. The first of these took place on 28 April when the lifeboat again assisted the sailing vessel *Albatros* which had set off for Yarmouth, but went aground in the entrance to Wells Channel whilst proceeding to sea under power. The lifeboat connected a tow and after a short while *Albatros* came off the bank under her own power, making her way back into Wells Harbour escorted by the lifeboat. Further services took place on 5 September, when *Doris M. Mann of Ampthill* brought in the yacht *Krign Storm*, and on 8 October she was called to the fishing vessel *Laura Jane*, of Blakeney, assisting both to safety.

After a quiet start to 2005, *Doris M. Mann of Ampthill* had a busy time in June, July and August. On 15 June, she launched to search for people thought to be in the water after a capsized sailing dinghy, fully rigged and loaded with personal belongings, had been found fifteen miles off from Sheringham. Despite an extensive search between Scolt Head and Blakeney Point, starting close inshore and working north, she failed to find anything and was stood down at 1.15 a.m. the following morning. Three days later, she was called into action again, launching to a small sailing dinghy reported to be in trouble outside Blakeney Harbour entrance and in danger of being swept out to sea. After launching at 10.23 p.m., *Doris M. Mann of Ampthill* found the vessel just over ten minutes later and verified that the reported casualty, the sailing vessel *Luney*, was in no immediate danger, all was well on board and so the lifeboat returned after a fruitless journey.

During the afternoon of 1 July 2005, *Doris M. Mann of Ampthill* launched to a small open boat whose two occupants were in difficulty off Blakeney. The boat's main outboard had failed and, with just a small outboard motor, it was making little headway against the tide. By 5 p.m. the

Doris M. Mann of Ampthill *on exercise in April 2005 off Wells Harbour. (Nicholas Leach)*

lifeboat was afloat and soon took the casualty in tow, proceeding to the safety of Morston Creek where the boat was moored. A week later, on 8 July, in force five winds and moderate to rough seas, the small sailing vessel *Lady Libra* requested assistance in entering Wells Harbour because of breaking swell on the bar. As the lifeboat put out at 7.20 p.m., reports were received of a medical casualty on another small sailing vessel, *Whistler*. The skipper of *Lady Libra* was happy to stand off and wait, so the lifeboat went to the aid of *Whistler*, onto which crewman Mark Frary was transferred and a tow and drogue were attached. *Whistler* was then towed to the quay by when the injured crew member was feeling better in calmer waters so the lifeboat returned to sea, transferred crewman Mark Frary to *Lady Libra*, and secured a tow to that vessel to bring her in. As soon as the second vessel was alongside the quay at 8.55 p.m., the coastguard requested the lifeboat proceed at full speed to a third casualty which was reported about ten miles east of the boathouse off Salthouse. At 9.45 p.m., the lifeboat was alongside the casualty, the yacht *Tamara* with one person onboard, which was on passage to Great Yarmouth and riding out the strong northerly winds close to the lee shore. As the vessel was in no apparent danger, the lifeboat returned to Wells to be rehoused and made ready for service.

After standing by on 20 August 2005 ready to launch to a fishing boat which went aground near Blakeney Harbour, when the coastguard and a local seal tour boat located the casualties and brought them to safety without lifeboat help, *Doris M. Mann of Ampthill* was called out two days later to another local fishing vessel, *Laura Jane*, which had lost steerage with two persons on board. With wind and swell steadily increasing during the evening, the fishing vessel had anchored ten miles to seaward of Blakeney Harbour to await assistance. The lifeboat launched in Holkham Bay at 6.20 p.m. in force six winds and proceeded directly towards the casualty. Meanwhile, another local fishing vessel, *Terry William*, took the casualty in tow and headed for Blakeney. At 7 p.m., the lifeboat took over the tow and brought the casualty toward Blakeney Harbour, where the vessel was moored allowing the lifeboat to return to Wells Harbour.

Throughout 2005, while the above rescues were being undertaken, various people connected with the station, led by Coxswain Allen Frary and Bridget Marshall, were preparing to mark

At the end of September, BBC TV covered the story of the anniversary of the 1880 disaster by filming a re-enactment of the events using the former Bembridge lifeboat Queen Victoria *(O.N. 112), a 34ft self-righter of similar design to* Eliza Adams *and now rebuilt for use around the country at fund-raising events. (Paul Russell)*

Lifeboat Operations Manager Peter Rainsford opens the proceedings on 29 October 2005 at the start of the memorial services to mark the 125th anniversary of the Eliza Adams *tragedy. Coxswain Allen Frary is on the far left with Station Chaplain Revd Tony Douglas on his left. (Nicholas Leach)*

the 125th anniversary of the capsizing of the station's first lifeboat *Eliza Adams* on 29 October 1880. A series of events to remember the tragedy, in which eleven of the thirteen lifeboatmen on board lost their lives, was organised. A service was held exactly to the hour that the disaster occurred with crew and officials from the station, together with supporters, well-wishers and descendents of the lifeboatmen lost in the tragedy, gathered at the station to remember the lifeboatmen who had given their lives. The descendants were welcomed to Wells by Coxswain Allen Frary and personnel from Wells lifeboat station, and then assembled at the lifeboat station at the end of Beach Road. Lifeboat Operations Manager Peter Rainsford read an account of the disaster recalling the events of that fateful day which had taken place within sight of the current lifeboat house. Following this, a lament was played on bagpipes by shorehelper Richard Dawson and, while this was played, the lifeboat crew led by Coxswain Frary boarded the lifeboat. Once on board, crew member Bridget Marshall read a poem that had appeared in *The People's Weekly Journal* of 13 November 1880, a couple of weeks after the disaster.

Following a minute's silence, impeccably observed by the large crowd of supporters, two maroons were fired, signalling the launch of both lifeboats. The *Mersey* set off for the harbour entrance, with Wells Station Chaplain Revd Tony Douglas on board, followed by the D class inflatable. At about 3.45 p.m., the lifeboat reached the position of the capsize where a service at sea was conducted by Revd Douglas with the crew taking it in turns to lay roses in memory of the lifeboatmen who gave their lives. Following the firing of two white flares, an RAF Sea King helicopter from Wattisham flew over the lifeboat house where descendants and supporters had the service at sea relayed to them via radio. The lifeboat then returned to harbour and moored at Wells Quay so the crew could go to the memorial on Beach Road for another service.

After the hymn 'Eternal Father Strong to Save' had been sung, an account of the disaster taken from *The People's Weekly Journal* of November 1880 was read to the crowd by Ian Clark,

The lifeboat crew on board the lifeboat Doris M. Mann of Ampthill *during the reading of the poem 'Weep for the Brave'. Left to right: Bob Smith (second coxswain), Revd Tony Douglas (partially hidden), Fred Whitaker, Greg Hewitt (deputy / second coxswain), Mark Frary, Bridget Marshall and Allen Frary (coxswain). (Nicholas Leach)*

The lifeboat crew drop roses over the side of Doris M. Mann of Ampthill *during the memorial service which was broadcast by radio to the lifeboat house where the relatives were assembled. On board are, left to right: Greg Hewitt, Michael Frary, Bob Smith, Fred Whitaker, Bridget Marshall, Coxswain Allen Frary, Mark Frary and Nicky King. On the canopy is the Revd Tony Douglas. (Nicholas Leach)*

Richard Cracknell opens the service at the lifeboat memorial, 29 October 2005. Left to right are Bob Smith, Michael Frary, Bridget Marshall, Greg Hewitt, Nicky King, Fred Whitaker, Mark Frary, Gary Wright, Ian Clarke (Chief Reporter from the Dereham and Fakenham Times), Coxswain Allen Frary, Peter Rainsford (Lifeboat Operations Manager), Rev Tony Douglas and Father Michael Simison. (Nicholas Leach)

chief reporter of the *Dereham and Fakenham Times*. Coxswain Frary then read another account of events, this one an eyewitness version by Captain Thomas Kew, one of the survivors. The Revd Douglas led the service of remembrance which began with Lifeboat Operations Manager Peter Rainsford reading the names of the thirteen crew members of *Eliza Adams* as Mrs Flossie Fairchild, one of the descendants of the two Eldson brothers who both lost their lives, laid a wreath at the memorial. At 5 p.m., the lifeboats returned to the lifeboat station to be recovered, after which crew and supporters gathered for the re-enactment of the inquest of 1880 at The Crown Hotel performed by the Wells Granary Players, a group of local actors.

Less than a month after the commemorations, *Doris M. Mann of Ampthill* was called out for real. On 20 November 2005, she went to the motor fishing vessel *Harriet Jane* from Blakeney with two people on board about twelve miles east-north-east of the lifeboat station. The fishing vessel was out pot hauling when her gearbox broke. Sheringham lifeboat *Manchester Unity of Oddfellows* (B-702) was already on exercise so the coastguard diverted them to *Harriet Jane* and tow the casualty back to Blakeney. Unfortunately just after the tow started, one of the lifeboat's two engines stopped working so *Doris M. Mann of Ampthill* was launched to take the tow over. After a low water launch in Holkham Bay at about 12.30 p.m., the lifeboat set off and met both boats north of Blakeney Harbour half an hour later with the Sheringham boat towing at six knots on the one engine. After getting a tow aboard, the fishing vessel's skipper said he would like to come to Wells. The tow was therefore diverted to Wells, where the lifeboat and casualty arrived at 1.45 p.m. but had to wait until 6.30 p.m. before there was enough water to get to the quay.

This kind of service represents the bread and butter of Wells lifeboat rescues and adds another figure to the already impressive tally. Between 1869, when the station was established by the RNLI, and 31 December 2005, the all weather lifeboats that have served Wells-next-the Sea have saved 172 lives and launched 419 times on service, and the station's inshore lifeboats have saved 179 lives in 367 launches. Six pulling and sailing lifeboats, ten motor lifeboats and ten inshore lifeboats have been operated by the station and protected all those who get into difficulty off the north Norfolk coast.

Appendices

Appendix 1. Lifeboat summary

On station	ON	Name Donor	Type Year built	Launches/ lives saved
1830–p.1850	—	[Not named] Norfolk Mariners Association	25' North Country 1804	?/?
1869–1880	—	*Eliza Adams* Gift Dr E. P. Adams, Bungay	33' Self-righter 1869	15/38
12.1880–88	—	*Charlotte Nicholls* Legacy of Miss Charlotte Nicholls, London	37' Self-righter 1880	1/5
8.1888–1895	198	*Baltic* Baltic Exchange	37' Self-righter 1888	3/0
7.1895–1913	375	*Baltic* Baltic Exchange	35'3" Cromer 1895	13/19
10.1913–16	425	*James Stevens No.8* Legacy of James Stevens, Birmingham	35' Liverpool 1899	2/0
9.1916–1936	665	*Baltic* Baltic Exchange	38' Liverpool 1916	21/12
2.1936–1945	780	*Royal Silver Jubilee 1910–1935* RNLI funds	32' Surf (M) 1935	43/23
7.1945–1965	850	*Cecil Paine* Legacy of A. Paine	35'6" Liverpool (M) 1945	47/20
6.1965–1990	982	*Ernest Tom Neathercoat* Legacy of E.T. Neathercoat plus RNLI funds	37' Oakley (M) 1965	85/16
3.7.1990–	1161	*Doris M. Mann of Ampthill* Legacy of Doris M. Mann, Ampthill, Beds	38' Mersey (M) 1990	

ON indicates Official Number, (M) indicates motor lifeboat

Inshore lifeboats

On Station	ON	Name	Type
1963–64	D-11	—	
1965	D-9	—	
1965	D-29	—	
1965–66	D-8	—	
1966–68	D-82	—	
1968–69	D-25	—	
1970–76	D-113	—	
5.1976–87	D-246	*Spirit of Rotary*	Zodiac Mk.II
1988–11.96	D-352	*Jane Ann*	16'3" Avon EA16
13.11.1996– 4.2006	D-512	*Jane Ann II*	16'3" Avon EA16
4.2006–	D-661	*Jane Ann III*	16'3" IB1

Appendix 2. Lifeboat details

First lifeboat (not named)

Years on station	1830–c. 1850
Record	No record of any launches
Donor	Local subscriptions and Norwich Mariners' Association
Type	'Greathead' or North Country non-self-righter, ten-oared
Built	1804, Henry Greathead, South Shields
Dimensions	Length 25ft, breadth 8ft 6in
Notes	Originally stationed at Cromer

Eliza Adams

Years on station	November 1869–1880
Record	15 launches, 38 lives saved
Donor	Penny Readings Lifeboat Fund, from Dr Adams, Bungay
Naming ceremony	Named on 12 November 1869 by the Countess of Leicester
Cost	£281
Type	Self-righting, ten-oared
Built	1869, Woolfe, Shadwell
Dimensions	Length 33ft, breadth 8ft 6in
Notes	Capsized on service 29.10.1880

Charlotte Nicholls

Years on station	December 1880–August 1888
Record	One launch, 5 lives saved
Donor	Legacy of Miss Charlotte Nicholls, Finsbury Park, London
Naming ceremony	Named 26 July 1882 by by Mrs Cocking, wife of executor of the late Miss Nicholls
Cost	£430
Type	Self-righting, twelve-oared
Built	1880, Woolfe, Shadwell
Dimensions	Length 37ft, breadth 9ft
Disposal	Sold locally 1889

Baltic

Years on station	August 1888–July 1895
Record	3 launches, no lives saved
Donor	Baltic Exchange Lifeboat Fund, presented by H. Karris Jackson, Esq
Cost	£563 6s 6d
Official Number	198
Type	Self-righting, twelve-oared
Year	1888
Builder	D. & W. Henderson, Partick, yard no. HE598
Dimensions	Length 37ft, breadth 8ft
Disposal	Broken up 1895

Baltic

Years on station	July 1895–October 1913
Record	13 launches, 19 lives saved
Donor	Baltic Exchange Lifeboat Fund
Cost	£450
Official Number	375
Type	Cromer, fourteen-oared
Built	1895, James Beeching, Great Yarmouth, yard no. B8
Dimensions	Length 35ft 3in, breadth 10ft 3in, depth
Disposal	Condemned and sold 1913

James Stevens No.8

Years on station	13 October 1913–September 1916
Record	Two launches, no lives saved
Donor	Legacy of Mr James Stevens, Birmingham
Cost	£544
Official Number	425
Type	Liverpool, ten/twelve-oared, twelve-oared with fifteen crew from 1904
Built	1899, James Beeching, Great Yarmouth, yard no.B11
Dimensions	Length 35ft, breadth 10ft 9in, depth 4ft 7in
Notes	Originally at Ardrossan from 1899 to 1913, where she launched seven times on service and saved forty-one lives; Reserve 9B 1913 to 1920
Disposal	Condemned and sold 1920

Baltic

Years on station	September 1916–February 1936
Record	21 launches, 12 lives saved
Donor	Baltic Exchange Lifeboat Fund
Cost	£2,235 5s 1d
Official Number	665
Type	Liverpool, fourteen-oared
Built	1916, Saunders, Cowes, yard no.S21
Dimensions	Length 38ft, breadth 10ft 9in, depth
Disposal	Sold out of service in December 1943 to H.L. Goodson, Aldeburgh

Doris M. Mann of Ampthill is recovered on the beach after exercise, 2004. The propeller and rudder arrangements of the 12m Mersey are clear in this photograph, with both protected in partial tunnels. (Nicholas Leach)

Royal Silver Jubilee 1910–1935

Years on station	6 February 1936–July 1945
Record	43 launches, 23 lives saved
Donor	Gift of Mrs E.W. Montford, JP, patron of Newcastle-under-Lyme Ladies Guild to commemorate the Silver Jubilee of King George V and Queen Mary
Naming ceremony	13 July 1936
Cost	£2,918 19s 11d
Official Number	780
Type	Surf motor
Built	1935, Groves & Guttridge, Cowes, yard no.G&G206
Dimensions	Length 32ft, breadth 9ft, depth
Engines	Twin 12hp Weyburn F.2 two-cylinder petrol driving Hotchkiss Cones
Disposal	Sold to KNZHRM, Netherlands, 1946. Served at Vlieland, Holland (KNZHRM) from 1946 to 1959, then sold out of service. Subsequent whereabouts unknown

Cecil Paine

Years on station	25 July 1945–June 1965
Record	47 launches, 20 lives saved
Donor	Legacy of Mr A.C. Paine
Cost	£7,462 0s 3d
Official Number	850
Type	Liverpool motor
Built	1945, Groves & Guttridge, Cowes, yard no.G&G418
Dimensions	Length 35ft 6in, breadth 10ft 8in, depth
Engines	Twin 18bhp Weyburn AE4 diesels, re-engined 1964 with twin 32hp Penguin diesels
Notes	Fitted with a single mast and carried two oars
Disposal	Sold 1972 to Portuguese LB Service

Ernest Tom Neathercoat

Years on station	June 1965–July 1990
Record	85 launches, 16 lives saved
Donor	Legacy of Mr E.T. Neathercoat, Horsham, together with RNLI Funds
Naming ceremony	8 July 1965 at Wells by HRH Princess Marina, Duchess of Kent
Cost	£34,000
Official Number	982, operational number 37–15
Type	Oakley self-righter
Built	1965, William Osborne, Littlehampton, yard no.WO982
Dimensions	Length 37ft, breadth 11ft 6in
Engines	Twin 52hp Ford Parsons Porbeagle 592E four-cylinder diesels
Notes	After being replaced at Wells, taken to Leggett's Bt Yd, Grimsby, for inspection, then served at North Sunderland on temporary station duty August 1990-August 1991, before being taken to RNLI Depot, Poole, for disposal
Disposal	Displayed at the National Boatbuilding Centre, Oulton Broad, Lowestoft, from 1992 to 1998. In 1998, moved to the car park at the end of Beach Road, Wells. In September 2000, she was again moved, this time to a farm not far from Wells for storage prior to restoration

Doris M. Mann of Ampthill

Years on station	13 July 1990–
Donor	Legacy of Doris M. Mann, Ampthill, Bedfordshire
Naming ceremony	17.7.1990 at Wells Quay by HRH the Duchess of Kent
Cost	£468,209
Official Number	1161, operational number 12–003
Type	Mersey
Built	1991, FBM Ltd, Cowes, yard no.1266
Dimensions	Length 38ft, breadth 12ft 6in, depth 6ft
Engines	Twin Caterpillar 3208T turbo-charged diesels
Notes	Aluminium hulled, one of eight Merseys to be so constructed

Appendix 3. Service summary

Eliza Adams Lifeboat

1872	Aug 27	Yacht *Stella*, of London, saved 7
		Brig *Criterion*, of Arbroath, saved 9
	Nov 11	Fishing lugger *Northumberland*, of Flamborough, gave assistance
1874	Mar 6	Schooner *Marie*, of St Valéry-en-Caux, saved 5
	Oct 22	Brig *Indien*, of Bordeaux, saved 6
1878	Sep 12	Fishing sloop *Sally*, of Wells, saved 4
1880	Oct 29	Brig *Sharon's Rose*, of Whitby, saved 7

Charlotte Nicholls Lifeboat

| 1883 | Oct 4 | Schooner *Emma*, of Jersey, saved 5 |

Baltic (first) Lifeboat

1898	Mar 23	Fishing smack *F.T.B.*, of Boston, saved 4
1900	Aug 4	Ketch *Hopewell*, of Lynn, saved 3
1901	Nov 14	Ketch *Lily*, of Grimsby, saved 2
1903	Sep 11	Ketch *Eliza Patience*, of Great Yarmouth, saved 2
1909	Apr 1	Ketch *Providence*, of Goole, saved 4
	Dec 1	Barge *Jane*, of London, landed 3
	22	Ketch barge *Davenport*, of Ipswich, saved barge and 4

Baltic (second) Lifeboat

1919	Aug 14	Fishing boat *Rock of Ages*, saved boat and 3
	Oct 9	Steamship *Urd*, of Swansea, saved 6
1921	Nov 3	Motor fishing boat *Boy Robert*, of Wells, escorted
1924	Sep 4	Steamship *Coniscrag*, of Glasgow, gave help
1934	Mar 2	Motor fishing boat *Tony*, of Wells, gave help
1935	Feb 25	Motor fishing boat *Tony*, of Wells, saved 3

Royal Silver Jubilee 1910–1935 Lifeboat

1936	Mar 26	Steamship *Boree*, of Caen, rendered assistance
	May 24	Motor cruiser *Water Nymph*, rendered assistance
	Sep 20	Motor vessel *Karanan*, of Rotterdam, stood by
	29	Motor vessel *Karanan*, gave help
	30	Motor vessel *Karanan*, gave help
1937	Feb 7	Motor fishing boat *Liberty*, of Wells, escorted
	July 24	Motor yacht *Gazeka*, of London, saved yacht and 6
	Nov 19	Auxiliary ketch *Elizabeth*, of Hamburg, landed 4
	Dec 8	Motor vessel *Helen Birch*, of Hull, gave help
1939	Dec 23	Fishing boat *Malvina*, of Wells, escorted
1940	Mar 1	Boat of steamship P.L.M. 25, of Rouen, saved boat
1941	Jan 15	Steamship *Faxfleet*, stood by and landed 7
	May 6	Steamship *Radstock*, of Bridgwater, gave help
	June 26	Aircraft, salved gear
	Nov 27	British aircraft, helped to save
1942	Jan 9	Steamship *Eastwood*, of London, stood by
	July 14	British Lancaster Bomber aircraft, saved 1
1944	Jan 10	HM Drifter 634, assisted to save drifter and 5
	Nov 3	War Department motor vessel *Caddel*, saved vessel and 5
	13	HM Landing Craft LC(T) 908, gave help

Cecil Paine Lifeboat

1947	Feb 9	Motor vessel *Spirality*, of London, stood by
1948	July 25	Royal Fleet Auxiliary tanker *Wave Commander*, of London, landed an injured man
1949	Jan 28	Motor fishing boat *Sally*, of Wells, saved boat and 2

	July 16	Royal Army Service Corps motor vessel *Fagin*, gave help
	Sep 30	Fishing boats *Spero* and *Blanche*, of Wells, escorted
1951	July 4	Nine fishing boats, of Wells, escorted
1954	Dec 9	Motor barge *Gold*, of Rochester, in tow of lifeboatRNLB *Foresters' Centenary*, of Sheringham, gave help
1955	May 18	Steamship *Zor*, of Istanbul, gave help and saved 5
1956	Mar 22	Motor fishing boat *Harvester*, of Wells, saved boat and 2
	May 28	Yacht *Wire*, of Glasgow, saved yacht and 1
	July 29	Yacht *Elleana*, of Great Yarmouth, saved yacht and 5
	Oct 31	Steamship *Eleanor Brooke*, of London, landed a doctor and the body of the master of steamship *Wimbledon*, of London
		RNLB *Foresters' Centenary*, of Sheringham, gave help
		RNLB *Foresters' Centenary*, of Sheringham, escorted lifeboat
1957	June 5	Converted ship's boat *Sailfish*, saved boat and 1
1961	July 14	Converted ship's boat *Boy John*, saved boat and 2

Lucy Lavers Reserve Lifeboat

1962	Sep 19	Motor cruiser Y811, saved cruiser

Cecil Paine Lifeboat

1963	May 18	Cabin cruiser *Seamus*, of Frinton, saved 2

Lucy Lavers Reserve Lifeboat

1963	July 15	Catamaran, of Brancaster, in tow of fishing boat, landed 3
	Nov 21	Four sprat boats *Cortina, Romulus, Remus* and *Leona*, of Sheringham, escorted
1964	Feb 9	Motor barge *Una*, of Oslo, gave help

Cecil Paine Lifeboat

1964	July 2	Fishing boat *Blanche*, of Wells, gave help
	Aug 19	Fishing boats *Blanche* and *Sally*, of Wells, escorted
	29	Sloop-yacht *Kiskadee*, gave help

Ernest Tom Neathercoat Lifeboat

1965	July 31	Yacht *Eljida*, of Hull, gave help
	Dec 28-29	Oil rig *Sea Gem*, stood by
1966	Sep 15	Yacht *Kylin*, saved yacht, a dog, and 1
1967	July 30	Motor fishing boat *Aline*, gave help and escorted
	Oct 31	Whelk boat *William Henry*, of Wells, escorted
	Dec 21	Fishing boat *Firth*, of Wells, gave help
1969	Jan 15	Aircraft, recovered wreckage
	May 21	'Hunter' Aircraft, recovered wreckage
	Oct 31	Fishing boat *Blanche*, of Wells, saved boat and 2
1971	Jan 26	Fishing boat LT.424, of Lowestoft, gave help
1972	Apr 10	Two fishing boats *Elizabeth* and *William Edward*, escorted boats
	May 2	Fishing boat *Sovereign*, of Brancaster, gave help
1973	Sep 16	Fishing vessel *Graceful Lady*, gave help
1974	June 6	Fishing boat *Blanche*, escorted boat
	Sep 3	Motor vessel *Nordenstedt*, of Hamburg, escorted boat
	Nov 16	Motor fishing vessel *Corsair*, saved boat and 5
1975	Dec 8	Motor barge *Lo-An*, gave help
1976	Sep 16	Motor vessel *Will Mary* in tow of motor vessel *Smit Lloyd 5*, escorted boats

Calouste Gulbenkian Reserve Lifeboat

1977	Jun 5	Fishing vessel *John B*, stood by

Ernest Tom Neathercoat Lifeboat

	Nov 11	Cabin cruiser *Niny II* in tow of fishing boat *Sleep Robber*, escorted bts
1978	July 5	Motor fishing vessel *Amerthyst*, of Wells, gave help
1979	Jan 31	Motor fishing vessel *Amerthyst*, of Wells, gave help

	Feb 15	Cargo vessel *Savinesti*, of Rumania, stood by
	Mar 1	Motor fishing vessel *Myndroom*, landed 3 bodies
	Sep 17	Motor fishing vessel *Four Brothers*, of Wells, gave help
	Dec 14	Fishing boats *Anne Isobella*, *Swan Ranger*, *Wild Wave*, and *William Edward*, escorted
1980	Apr 19	Cabin cruiser *Nagram*, stood by
	May 3	Yacht *Bess*, gave help
	Nov 14	Fishing boat *Four Brothers*, gave help
1981	Feb 9	Fishing vessels *Isabelle Kathleen* and *Wild Wave*, escorted vessels
	Nov 20	Motor fishing vessel *Sarah K*, saved 4

Calouste Gulbenkian Relief Lifeboat

1983	Jan 3	Fishing vessel *Sea Witch*, of Shoreham, gave help
	Apr 11	Motor fishing vessel *Isabelle Kathleen*, of Wells, escorted vessel
		Ex-tug *Dockman*, gave help
	Jun 25	Motor cruiser *Osprey*, saved boat

Ernest Tom Neathercoat Lifeboat

	Sep 10	Motor cruiser *Mi-Lady Jill*, escorted boat
1984	Jan 19	Motor fishing vessel *Four Brothers*, of Wells, escorted vessel
1985	May 5	Motor cruiser *Thorntree*, gave help
1986	Aug 29	Fishing vessel *Nicholas*, gave help
	Nov 21	Fishing vessels *Kenneth William* and *Mor-Nita*, escorted vessels

Calouste Gulbenkian Relief Lifeboat

1987	July 29	Yacht *Lesintrigants*, of Netherlands, saved boat and 5
	Aug 24	Yacht *Free Spirit*, escorted vessel
	Dec 5	Fishing vessel *Mor-Nita*, stood by
1988	Feb 1	Fishing vessel *Viking*, of King's Lynn, craft brought in- gave help

Ernest Tom Neathercoat Lifeboat

	June 27	Cabin cruiser *La Mancha*, saved boat and 3
	Nov 26	Fishing vessel *Valerie Marilyn*, craft brought in- gave help
1989	Mar 28	Motor fishing vessel *Three Brothers*, of Wells, gave help
	July 30	Yacht *Sharon*, escorted
		Yacht *Scorpios Dream*, escorted
		Motor fishing vessel *Sea Eagle*, escorted
		Yacht *Meg*, in tow of RNLB *Manchester Unity of Odd Fellows*, of Sheringham, escorted
		Yachts *Serena* and *Martlet*, in tow of RNLB *Ruby and Arthur Reed II*, of Cromer, escorted
	Sep 14	Yacht *Amber Crest*, in tow of inshore lifeboat D-352, of Wells, escorted boats

Doris M. Mann of Ampthill Lifeboat

1990	July 23	Motor fishing vessel *Sheena Mackay*, saved boat and 2
	Dec 1	Motor yacht *Omega P*, landed 4 and gave help
1991	June 15	Yacht *Leveret*, saved boat and 3
	July 12	Catamaran *Witham Wandrer*, with machinery failure, gave help
	Oct 16	Fishing vessel *Mor-Nita*, gave help
		Fishing vessel *Cerealia*, saved boat and 2
1992	Apr 2	Cabin cruiser *Havoc*, escorted boat
	May 28	Yacht *Witch Hunter*, escorted
	June 18	Fishing vessel *Minerva* with fouled propeller, gave help
	18	Seven fishing vessels in adverse conditions, escorted
	28	Motor boat *Razzmataz*, landed 3 and saved boat
	July 4	Catamaran *Eloise*, stood by
		Six fishing vessels, stood by boats
		Yacht *Jean Van Gent*, escorted yacht
1993	Feb 17	Yacht *Heavy Metal*, escorted boat
	July 5	Motor cruiser *Rocking Horse*, gave help
	25	Yacht *Starlight Speshull*, saved boat and 5

Marine Engineer Relief Lifeboat [on passage]

July 25   Yacht *Starlight Speshull*, in tow of *Doris M. Mann of Ampthill*, escorted

Doris M. Mann of Ampthill Lifeboat

		31	Yacht *Aubie*, saved boat and 4
	Aug	5	Catamaran *Pussy Galore*, assisted to save boat and 4
	Sep	6	Fishing vessel *Pintail*, gave help
		12	Sailing barge *Albatros*, escorted boat
1994	June	12	Body in sea, landed a body
	July	24	Rubber dinghy *Cambridge Divers*, saved boat and 1
	Sep	3	Motor cruiser *Longhope*, gave help
1995	Aug	13	Fishing vessel *Katherine Lucy*, two persons landed and craft brought in
1996	May	5	Yacht *Condor*, four persons and craft brought in
	June	1	Yacht *Tara*, saved craft
		21	Yacht *Venture*, escorted craft
	Aug	4	Cabin cruiser *Starry Vere*, gave help
		8	Cabin crusier *Fair Kate*, three persons and craft brought in
	Sep	2	Fishing vessel *Ma Freen*, three persons and craft brought in
		16	Fishing vessel *Mornita*, two persons and craft brought in
	Oct	31	Yacht *March*, gave help
	Nov	17	Fishing vessel *Remus*, saved craft and 2
1997	Aug	14	Yacht *Rose of Otford*, one person and craft brought in
			Yacht *Harlequin*, escorted craft
		17	Catamaran *Alleycat*, gave help
1998	July	17	Yacht *She's Chic*, gave help

Peggy and Alex Caird Relief Lifeboat

Aug	11	Yacht *Piper*, One person and vessel towed in
	24	Motor *Fairlie Knackered*, stood by
Oct	11	Fishing vessel *Buzzard*, escorted vessel

Doris M. Mann of Ampthill Lifeboat

		31	Yacht *Marynette*, one person and yacht towed in
1999	Feb	20	Yacht *Wren*, two people and craft brought in
	Apr	3	Yacht *Stella Maris*, saved craft and 2
		9	Fishing vessel *Shangri-la*, three people and craft brought in
		11	Fishing vessel *La Belle Helene*, two people and craft brought in
	July	18	Powerboat *Jasmay*, one person and craft brought in
	Aug	7	Power boat *Katie Shannon*, landed 2 and craft saved
		13	Fishing vessel *Northern Prince*, five people and craft brought in
		15	Sick man on merchant vessel *Hoo Falcon*, gave help
	Sep	4	Yacht *Nereid*, landed 5 and craft brought in
		10	Fishing vessel *Mor-Nita*, two people and craft brought in
	Dec	16	Powerboat *Samphire*, assisted to recover a body
		22	Body in sea, landed a body
2000	Sep	2	Yacht *Candy,* saved craft and 3
2001	May	21	Fishing vessel *Isabelle Kathleen*, three people and craft brought in
	June	5	Yacht *Shamsuddin*, one person and craft brought in
	July	19	Motor cruiser *Siesta Time*, gave help
		29	Fishing vessel *Laura Jane*, three people and craft brought in
		31	Merchant vessel *Allegonda*, two people and craft brought in
	Aug	31	Yacht *Black Fox*, three people and craft brought in
	Sep	8	Yacht *Costley*, saved craft and 2
	Dec	28	Person cut off by the tide, stood by
2002	Jan	9	Fishing vessel *Zuiderzee*, saved vessel and 3
	Apr	26	Motor vessel *Albatros*, landed craft and 11
	May	18	Yacht *Lady Gurtrude*, landed craft and 1
	June	4	Yacht *Amurus*, craft brought in
		8	Fishing vessel *Desert Moon*, craft brought in
		9	Barge *De-Hoop 3,* escorted

	July 1	Yacht *Sing High*, escorted
	Aug 31	Power boat *Jennifer*, craft brought in
2003	May 12	Fishing vessel *Laura Jane*, craft brought in
	May 24	Yacht *Rambling Rose*, gave help
		Fishing vessel *Ma Freen*, craft brought in
	July 2	Yacht *Olympiad*, craft brought in
	4	Motor vessel *Hambedon*, gave help
	9	Fishing vessel *Laura Jane*, saved craft and landed 2
	27	Yacht *Black Duck*, gave help
	Aug 17	Fishing vessel *John Barry*, craft brought in

Royal Shipwright Relief Lifeboat

	Sep 1	Sailing dinghy, assisted to save 2
	22	Yacht *Tequila*, landed 4 and craft brought in
	26	Fishing vessel *Seagull*, craft brought in
	Oct 21	Fishing vessel *Wash Princess*, craft brought in

Doris M. Mann of Ampthill Lifeboat

2004	28 Apr	Motor vessel *Albatros*, gave help
	23 May	Yacht *Cygnus*, two persons and craft brought in
	5 Sep	Yacht *Krign Storm*, three persons and craft brought in
	8 Oct	Fishing vessel *Laura Jane*, two persons and craft brought in
2005	July 1	Motor boat, persons and craft brought in
	8	Yacht *Lady Libra*, two persons and craft brought in
		Yacht *Whistler*, two persons and craft brought in
	24	Sailing dinghy *Olivia Jane*, saved craft
		Barge *Annie May*, three persons and craft brought in
	Aug 22	Fishing vessel *Laura Jane*, three persons and craft brought in
	Oct 8	Yacht *Lady Elsie*, landed 3 and craft
	Nov 20	Fishing vessel *Harriet Jane*, two persons and craft brought in

Inshore lifeboat services

1964	May 1	Yacht *Skate*, gave help
1965	June 13	Persons cut off by tide, saved 2
	Aug 1	Yacht, gave help
	8	Dinghy, saved dinghy and 2
	Dec 15	Fishing boat *Leona*, landed inj man
1966	Apr 6	Men marooned in marshes, landed 2
	Sep 15	Yacht *Kylin*, stood by and escorted
1967	May 31	Motor fishing boat *Firth*, gave help
	June 18	Canoe, saved 1
1968	Aug 31	Sailing dinghy, gave help
1969	Aug 28	Boat, saved 8
		Persons cut off by tide, landed 5
1970	May 21	Children stranded by tide, landed 2
	June 19	Persons cut off by tide, saved 3
1971	May 9	Persons cut off by tide, saved 13
	June 20	Motor cruiser *John Kay*, in tow of RNLB *Foresters' Centenary*, gave help
	Aug 1	Speedboat *Miss Conduct*, saved boat and 4
1973	Aug 7	Sailing dinghy, saved dinghy and 2
	Sep 6	Cruiser *Bonnie and Clyde*, esc
1974	June 30	Persons cut off by tide, landed 4
	July 17	Persons cut off by tide, stood by
	Aug 10	Dinghy, saved 2
	15	Cabin cruiser *Vigo II*, saved 4
		Persons cut off by tide, landed 4 (and dog)
	29	Persons cut off by tide, gave help
	Sep 22	Yacht *Albebaran*, landed 2
		Dinghy, gave help
1975	May 26	Yacht *Red Queen*, saved yacht and 2
	June 8	Persons cut off by tide, landed 6
	Aug 23	Yacht *Peggy*, landed 6
1976	July 26	Motor cruiser *Lovely Day*, gave help
	Aug 4	Two bathers, gave help
1977	July 19	Yacht *Shamrock*, in tow of fishing boat *Sea Queen II*, escorted
	20	Yacht, gave help
	Oct 23	Three persons cut off by tide, landed 3
1978	May 1	Sailing dinghy *Miranda*, gave help
	June 18	Fourteen persons cut off by tide, landed 14
	July 9	Yacht *Millow Maid*, saved 3
	12	Yacht *L'Escargot*, saved 1
	16	Four persons cut off by tide, stood by
	26	Person cut off by tide, gave help
	Aug 21	Yacht *Phoenix*, gave help
	26	Person cut off by tide, gave help
	28	Rubber dinghy, saved boat and landed 3
		Rubber dinghy, saved boat and 4
1979	Apr 22	Missing crewman from sunken fishing vessel *Concorde II*, landed a body
	July 9	Yacht *Ombla*, landed 1
	Aug 6	Rubber dinghy, saved boat and 1
	Sep 15	Rubber dinghy, saved boat and 5
	30	Sailing dinghy, landed 2
1980	May 23	Yacht *Stella Maris II*, gave help
	July 20	Motor boat *Electric Blue*, escorted
	Aug 10	Speedboat *Rich Jewel*, escorted
	17	Motor boat, escorted boat
	Sep 15	Dinghy, saved boat
1981	May 10	Catamaran *Midnight Fire*, gave help
		Catamaran *Midnight Fire*, escorted boat

	July 24	Rubber dinghy, stood by
		Rubber dinghy, landed 2
	Aug 20	Yacht *Nancy Stuart*, landed 2
1982	Aug 10	Sailboard, saved board and 1
	Oct 29	Two youths cut off by tide, saved 2
1983	July 8	Three boys cut off by tide, saved 3
	Sep 11	Four sailboards, gave help
1984	June 17	Speed-boat, saved boat and landed 2
	Aug 5	Yacht *Sundowner of Gilkicker,* saved boat and landed 3
1985	Apr 21	Yacht *Louise III*, landed 2
	July 29	Yacht *Helmspray III,* gave help
	Aug 5	Sailboard, saved board and 1
1986	May 23	Speedboat *Magician*, gave help
	June 29	Two persons cut off by tide, landed 1 and landed a body
	July 17	Three men cut off by tide, landed 3
	Aug 29	Fishing vessel *Nicholas*, gave help
1987	June 8	Persons cut off by tide, landed 1
	27	Yacht *Sea Dog*, craft brought in – gave help
	July 20	Persons cut off by tide, landed 5
	Aug 6	Motor boat *Isabel*, saved bt and 4
1988	Mar 24	Sailboard, gave help
	July 24	Motor fishing vessel *Two Sisters*, gave help
	Aug 25	Sailboard, gave help
	28	Persons cut off by the tide, saved 2
	Sep 12	Sailboard, gave help
	Oct 22	Fishing vessel *Three Brothers*, saved boat and 2
1989	May 3	Yacht *Juggler*, gave help
	7	Sailboard, gave help
	June 26	Persons cut off by the tide, gave help
	July 6	Persons cut off by the tide, gave help
	20	Persons cut off by the tide, saved 2
	21	Persons in danger of drowning
	23	Persons cut off by the tide, gave help
	30	Five yachts, escorted
		Sailboards, stood by
		Motor boat, escorted
	Aug 22	Bather, gave help
	Sep 10	Persons cut off by the tide, landed 4
	14	Yacht *Amborcrest*, gave help
1990	Apr 25	Persons cut off by the tide, saved 2
	29	Persons cut off by the tide, saved 3
	July 12	Persons cut off by the tide, saved 3
	Aug 2	Persons cut off by the tide, saved 3
	3	Swimmer, gave help
	18	Swimmers, saved 4
	Sep 8	Sailboard, saved board and 1
		Persons cut off by the tide, saved 2
	19	Persons stranded, landed 2
	Oct 7	Sailboard, saved board and 1
	14	Persons stranded, saved (also a dog) 6
1991	Apr 1	Catamaran capsized, saved boat and 2
	May 27	Catamaran, saved crew
1992	May 3	Persons cut off by tide, saved 2
	3	Persons cut off by tide, others coped
	June 9	Auxiliary yacht, gave help
	28	Small open power boat, gave help
		Small fishing vessel swamping, esc
	30	Persons cut off by flood tide, saved 1
	July 5	Sailboard, saved 1
	11	Capsized sailing dinghy, landed dy
	30	Persons cut off by flood tide, saved 2
		Persons cut off by flood tide, saved 2

	Aug 13	Sailboard, others coped
	22	Capsized sailing dinghy, saved dinghy
	25	Inflatable in adverse conditions, saved casualty and 2
	Sep 8	Small fishing vessel with leak and swamping, others coped
	Oct 9	Persons cut off by flood tide, landed 1
	17	Large open power boat with machinery failure, landed
1993	May 30	Yacht *Bill and Tot*, escorted boat
	June 18	Three persons (and a dog) cut off by tide, saved a dog and 3
	July 25	Sailing dinghy *Deep Blue*, saved boat
	Aug 5	Cat *Pussy Galore*, asstd to saved boat and 3
1994	May 31	Two persons cut off by tide, landed 2
	June 5	Sailing dinghy, gave help
	July 24	Three persons cut off by tide, landed 3
1995	9	Motor cruiser *Southern Trades*, saved 4
	16	Cabin cruiser *Hippo*, gave help
	16	Two persons cut off by tide, two persons brought in
	Aug 10	Five persons cut off by tide, saved 5
	19	Sick man onboard motor cruiser *Daisy May*, landed a sick man
	Nov 10	Man brought ashore from fishing vessel *Gabrielle* for compassionate reasons
1996	Feb 18	Two persons cut off by tide, two persons brought in
	Apr 23	Motor cruiser *Blue Lancer*, gave help
	May 5	Yacht *Condor*, gave help
	June 1	Yacht *Tara*, gave help
	21	Yacht *Venture*, escorted craft
	21	Yacht *Ginette*, gave help
	23	Three persons cut off by tide, saved 3
	July 6	Rowing boat, two persons, a dog and craft brought in
	11	Motor cruiser *Electric Dream*, four persons brought in
	12	Fire on nature conservancy area, took out fire brigade personnel
	Sep 14	Man cut off by tide, saved 1
	Nov 5	Trimaran *Tribal Dancer*, two persons and craft brought in
1997	July 27	Sailboard, saved board and 1
	Aug 5	Yacht *Penelope Jane*, two people and craft brought in
	13	Yacht *Rose of Otford*, gave help
	15	Eight persons cut off by tide, landed 8
	16	Ten persons cut off by tide, landed 10
	18	Catamaran *Alleycat,*, gave help
		Two persons cut off by tide, saved 2
		Three persons cut off by tide, saved 3
	Oct 1	Three sailboards, landed 3 and three boards brought in
1998	July 7	Five persons cut off by tide, three people brought in and saved 1
	Aug 2	Motor boat, saved craft, a dog and 2
	9	Seven persons cut off by tide, saved 7
	13	Sailing dinghy, craft saved
	16	Yacht *Christina 2*, gave help
		Yacht *Christina 2*, landed 3 and craft brght in
	17	Two people cut off by tide, landed 2
	21	Sailing dinghy, landed 2 and craft brought in
		Canoe, landed 1 and craft brought in

	Aug 24	Sailboard, saved board and 1
	Oct 31	Yacht *Marynette*, gave help
1999	Apr 12	Sailboard, one person and board brought in
	May 3	Two persons and dog cut off by tide, landed 2 and dog
	16	Yacht *Christina*, landed 2
	June 26	Eight people cut off by tide, saved 8
	July 10	Three people cut off by tide, saved 3
	20	Sailing dinghy *Pinochio*, saved craft and 1
	24	Two people cut off by tide, landed 2
	26	Three people cut off by tide, landed 3
		One person cut off by tide, landed 1
	29	Two children cut off by tide, landed 2
	Aug 1	Inflatable dinghy, saved craft and 2
	11	Two people cut off by tide, landed 2
	18	Power boat *Right Charlie*, two people and craft brought in
	24	Four people cut off by tide, landed 4
	27	Six people cut off by tide, landed 6
	30	Two people cut off by tide, landed 2
	Sep 4	Yacht *Nereid*, gave help
	5	Missing person, landed 1
	Oct 26	Three people cut off by tide, landed 3
	Dec 16	Powerboat *Samphire*, assisted to recover body
	17	Powerboat *Samphire*, recovered wreckage
2000	Jan 29	Sailboard, saved and 1
	Feb 20	Two people and two dogs cut off by tide, landed 2
	Mar 3	Sailing dinghy, landed 1
		Sailboard, one person and board brought in
	May 27	Sailboard, landed 1 and craft brought in
	29	Two people cut off by tide, landed 2
	31	Phosphorous shells, gave help
	Aug 29	Two people and a dog cut off by tide, landed 2 and a dog
	Sep 2	Yacht *Candy*, assisted to save 3
	Nov 3	Powerboat *Red Rimmer*, saved boat
	20	Yacht *Cavatana II*, one person and craft brought in

2001	Feb 25	Kiteboard, landed 1 and board brought in
	July 8	Fishing vessel *Janet Christine*, three people and craft brought in
	Aug 8	Kitesurfer, gave help
	22	Five people and dog in danger of being carried away by tide, saved a dog and 5
	27	Swimmers, life saved 1
	Oct 14	Two people cut off by the tide, landed 2
	Dec 28	Person cut off by the tide, landed 1
2002	Apr 26	Sailboard, saved board and landed 1
	Aug 7	Persons cut off by tide, six persons brought in
	11	Motor boat *Hannah*, gave help
	Sep 1	Swimmer, one person brought in
	Nov 24	Motor boat, gave help
2003	Apr 9	Stranded person, stood by
	May 24	Yacht *Rambling Rose*, stood by
	July 19	Persons cut off by tide, five persons brought in
	Aug 10	Motor boat, escorted
	Oct 11	Cabin cruiser *Vee Express*, three brought in
	18	Canoes, gave help
		Canoes, landed canoe and 1
2004	Mar 4	Two persons cut off by tide, landed 2 and dog
	May 23	Yacht *Cygnus*, three persons and craft brought in
	June 28	Yacht *Sulli Suli*, one person and craft brought in
	30	Rowing boat, landed 4
	July 29	Rowing dinghy, landed 2
	Aug 14	Persons missing, assisted to save persons
		Persons missing, assisted to save persons
	30	Sailboard, saved board and 1
	Sep 26	Fishing vessel *Pathfinder*, landed an injured person
2005	Jan 1	Swimmer, one person brought in
	15	Motor boat *Happy Hooker*, gave help
	July 10	Persons cut off, two persons brought in
	23	Motor boat *Ivor Biggaboat*, landed 3
	Aug 10	Rubber dinghy, landed 3 and craft
	21	Persons cut off by tide, landed 2

The *ARGO* eight-wheel-drive vehicle, supplied in 2001 to fulfil a number of roles at the station. Powered by a 20hp engine, it can launch and recover the ILB at low water, assist in searches along the shore line, and transport crew and shore helpers if required. (Nicholas Leach)

Appendix 4. Personnel summary

Honorary Secretaries

Thomas Garwood	1869–71
Thomas Garwood, Jnr	1871–75
F.B. Southgate	1875–80
Rev J. Pilling	1880–83
Capt John Loynes	1883
E.B. Loynes	1883–95
Herbert E. Loynes	1895–1939
E.W. Rose	1939–40
Dr E.W. Hicks	1940–69
Lieut David J Case, RNVR	1969–94
Richard T. Cracknell	1994–2004
Peter H. Rainsford	2004–

Coxswains

Richard Smith	1869–75
H. Hinson	1875–79
Capt Robert William Elsdon	1879–80
Horace Hinson	1880–95
William Crawford	1895–1905
Thomas Stacey	1905–17
William Edward Grimes	1917–33
Theodore T.L. Nielsen	1933–47
William Rushmore Cox	1947–12.59
David James Cox	1.1.1960–86
Anthony T. Jordan	1986–89
Graham Basil Walker★	1.3.1989–97
Allen D. Frary★	1997–

Herbert Loynes, longest serving honorary secretary.

Second Coxswains

James Dunn	1869–79
John Elsdon	1879–80
William Crawford	1881–87
R. Stacey	1887–?
T. Stacey	1899–1905
C. Wordingham	1905–08
W. Watson	1908–12
Herbert Fuller	1912–16
Charles Edward Wordingham	1916–25
Theodore T. L. Neilsen	1925–33
William Rushmore Cox	1933–47
William E. Cooper	1947–60
Francis R. Taylor DSM	1960–71
Anthony T. Jordan	1971–86
John Nudds	1986–87
Graham Basil Walker	1987–89
Allen Frary	1989–97
Robert Smith	1997–

Mechanics

James Robert Cox	1936–64
(p.t.1936-48, f.t.1948-64)	
Albert Court	1964–82
Graham Basil Walker★	1982–97
Allen Frary★	1997–

★Joint Coxswain/Mechanic

Head Tractor Drivers

S.A. Abel	1936–38
Reginald Herbert Aylmer	1938–57
Leonard Alfred Reeve	1957–60
George Lenard John Read	1960–88
Philip Charles Eaglen	1988–

Assistant Tractor Drivers

Derek John Lack	1946–56
Frederick John Painter	1956–58
G.L.J. Read	1959–60
Russell Kenneth Randall	1960–83
Philip Charles Eaglen	1983–88
Desmond Paul Wright	1988–

Appendix 5. What became of the lifeboats?

Baltic (ON.665)

The station's last pulling lifeboat, Baltic, *was sold out of service in December 1943 to H.L. Goodson, of Aldeburgh, Suffolk. What became of her then is unknown, but by the early 1950s she had moved to the South Coast and been converted into the ketch* Fidelis, *based at Axmouth, under the ownership of R. Redvers Lewis. By the mid-1950s, having been acquired by J.V. Martyn, she was renamed* Marvin *and, in 1954, was fitted with twin 17bhp four-cylinder Morris engines. Between the 1950s and the 1980s, little is known of her whereabouts, but by the late 1980s she had moved to Southampton. In 1994, she was moored in the river Itchen at Northam, Southampton, with a cabin added. She has been in Southampton since then. In October 2003, she was at Smiths Quay Boatyard, on the river Itchen, Southampton, and had been given the name* Baltic *back. (Nicholas Leach)*

Royal Silver Jubilee 1910–35 (ON.780)

Royal Silver Jubilee 1910–35 was given by the RNLI to the north Dutch lifeboat society, KNZHRM, for use in Holland as a lifeboat. She was needed to help with the shortage of lifeboats following the wartime occupation by the Nazis. She served at Terschelling from 1946 to 1955, and was then sold in 1955. What became of her after service in the Netherlands is unknown.

Cecil Paine (ON.850)

Cecil Paine *was sold out of service in 1972 to the lifeboat service in Portugal, where she has been based ever since. She was renamed* Patreo-Joao-Rangel, *but has been retired at Sesimbra. (Tony Moore)*

Ernest Tom Neathercoat (ON.982)

After leaving service at Wells, Ernest Tom Neathercoat *was sent to North Sunderland where she was stationed from August 1990 to July 1991, launching eight times on service. She was then stored at the RNLI depot in Poole until April 1992, when she was taken to the National Boat Building Centre for display in the car park with 'Relief' painted on her stern but otherwise unaltered. In 1998, she returned to Wells and was placed on display in the car park at the end of Beach Road. In 2000, she was moved to a farm (as pictured) not far from Wells and stored, pending restoration. (Nicholas Leach)*

Other titles published by Tempus

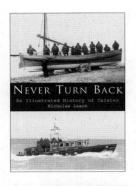

Never Turn Back An Illustrated History of Caister Lifeboats
NICHOLAS LEACH

The Caister lifeboat station is one of the most famous in the country, owing largely to the well-publicised life-saving exploits of the town's nineteenth-century lifeboat men and the tragedy that befell them in 1901, when their lifeboat, *Beauchamp*, capsized, trapping the crew beneath. Nine men were killed. This book takes a detailed look at all aspects of the lifeboat station at Caister, from its establishment in the first half of the nineteenth century to the stationing of the lifeboat, *Bernard Matthews*.

0 7524 2146 8

Cromer Lifeboats
NICHOLAS LEACH AND PAUL RUSSELL

Since 1804, a lifeboat has been stationed at Cromer ready to go to the aid of ships in distress off the Norfolk coast and to help people in difficulty in the dangerous waters of the North Sea. The coxswains and crews who have manned the Cromer lifeboat have a record of gallantry second to none, and are famous for their daring rescues and lifesaving exploits over two centuries. This comprehensive book which, for the first time in one volume, encompasses the complete history of the station from its establishment up to the present day.

0 7524 3197 8

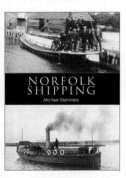

Norfolk Shipping
MICHAEL STAMMERS

The late eighteenth century saw the growth of steam ships and the gradual decline of traditional sailing craft. Norfolk has, though, been a haven for craft such as the fishing vessels that once used the harbour at Great Yarmouth. *Norfolk Shipping* is illustrated with 200 images of just some of the craft that have plied both the North Sea off the coast and inland to the Broads and along the county's main rivers.

0 7524 2757 1

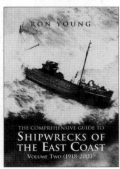

Shipwrecks of the East Coast Volume Two 1918–2003
RON YOUNG

The number of ships that have been wrecked along the coasts of Britain is huge and, despite the advent of radar and Global Positioning Satellites, wrecks still occur. In this comprehensive volume, covering the period from 1918 to 2003, Ron Young, an experienced diver, catalogues the history of the ships that have been wrecked along England's East Coast, giving co-ordinates and dimensions as well as describing the marine life and wrecks to be found on the seabed along this busy and treacherous stretch of coastline.

0 7524 2798 9

If you are interested in purchasing other books published by Tempus, or in case you have difficulty finding any Tempus books in your local bookshop, you can also place orders directly through our website

www.tempus-publishing.com